A Hymn to Life

A Hymn to Life
Shame Has to Change Sides

GISÈLE PELICOT

with Judith Perrignon

Translated from the French by
Natasha Lehrer and Ruth Diver

THE BODLEY HEAD
LONDON

1 3 5 7 9 10 8 6 4 2

The Bodley Head, an imprint of Vintage, is part of the Penguin Random House group of companies

Vintage, Penguin Random House UK, One Embassy Gardens,
8 Viaduct Gardens, London SW11 7BW

penguin.co.uk/vintage
global.penguinrandomhouse.com

First published by The Bodley Head in 2026
First published in French by Flammarion in 2026

Copyright © Gisèle Pelicot 2026
English translation copyright © Natasha Lehrer and Ruth Diver 2026

The moral right of the copyright holders has been asserted

Penguin Random House values and supports copyright. Copyright fuels creativity, encourages diverse voices, promotes freedom of expression and supports a vibrant culture. Thank you for purchasing an authorised edition of this book and for respecting intellectual property laws by not reproducing, scanning or distributing any part of it by any means without permission. You are supporting authors and enabling Penguin Random House to continue to publish books for everyone. No part of this book may be used or reproduced in any manner for the purpose of training artificial intelligence technologies or systems. In accordance with Article 4(3) of the DSM Directive 2019/790, Penguin Random House expressly reserves this work from the text and data mining exception.

Set in 14.2/17 pt Fournier MT Pro
Typeset by Six Red Marbles UK, Thetford, Norfolk
Printed and bound in Great Britain by Clays Ltd, Elcograf S.p.A.

The authorised representative in the EEA is Penguin Random House Ireland,
Morrison Chambers, 32 Nassau Street, Dublin D02 YH68

A CIP catalogue record for this book is available from the British Library

HB ISBN 9781847928962
TPB ISBN 9781847928979

Penguin Random House is committed to a sustainable future
for our business, our readers and our planet. This book is made
from Forest Stewardship Council® certified paper.

ONE

I always set the table for breakfast the night before. I put out coffee cups, plates, cutlery, napkins, pots of honey and jam. Almost as a way of reaching across the hours of darkness that I fear, of proclaiming the harmony of the day to come. Then all there is to do in the morning is get out the butter, put on the kettle, and wait for the smell of coffee and toast to fill the air. All will be well.

That evening, as usual, I got everything ready. Even Dominique's clothes. Let's call him Dominique. I never used to call him that, I preferred affectionate nicknames – Doumé, Mino – but afterwards I didn't know what to call him any more. I called him Monsieur. Monsieur Pelicot. Now that it is time to tell our story, I have decided to use his first name. I put out a pair of bottle-green corduroy trousers and a pink Lacoste polo shirt the children had given him.

We had to be at the police station the following morning; the appointment was at 9.30. After we woke up, we drank our coffee and listened to the news on RTL. The global Covid pandemic had picked up with a vengeance and another lockdown was in force. I looked up at the sky through the kitchen window facing me. It was going to be a lovely day, so I suggested a long walk after lunch as a way of defying the government's restrictions, and as an antidote to the morning's summons. Dominique sat opposite me and said nothing. I reminded him it was November 2nd; my brother, Michel, would have been sixty-nine today. He sighed and said he didn't like November, it was never a good month, no doubt an allusion to all the bills and notices of unpaid invoices that were about to come in. My ghosts and our money problems hung there between us in the kitchen for a moment. But we had always lived with them. And in a way, they had brought us closer. Dominique went to take a shower while I cleared the table. As we were about to leave, he pulled on a jacket that did not go at all with the outfit I had put together for him. I told him so, and he shrugged. We took my car. He drove us to the Carpentras police station.

Two months earlier, I had been staying with our daughter, Caroline, and her husband, Pierre, outside Paris, looking after my grandson until school started, and we had gone to spend the weekend at their holiday home on the Ile de Ré, off the Atlantic coast of France. That's where I was when Dominique called me sounding unusually agitated. He stammered something about having lost his mobile, he needed a code to activate the new one he had just bought to replace it, he'd had it sent to my number. I gave him the code, but everything about this usually methodical and organised man seemed suddenly in disarray. When he came to pick me up at the station a few days later he looked gaunt. We got home and he burst into tears. He said he couldn't bear to lose me. I thought immediately of my father's grief when my mother died. Dominique sat beside me, shaking with sobs, and I was unable to console him. I feared he might be ill, that his cancer might have returned to take him away for good.

When Dominique finally confessed to me that the previous week he had done something foolish at the Carpentras branch of the Leclerc supermarket – he'd been caught by a security guard filming under three women's skirts, ended up at the police station and had his phone and computer seized – I was upset but I was also, in a way, almost relieved. It was terrible to think of my husband stalking these women, unbearable to imagine him as an offender, but it could have been so much worse. This was not irreversible. My fears were measured on a different scale: only death really frightened me.

So I told him that we would keep the incident between us; I wouldn't tell the children, so as not to hurt them. And I wasn't about to give up on him, but he absolutely had to apologise to the women he had filmed, and see a therapist. There wouldn't be a next time, because if there was, I would leave. 'I promise you,' he said, 'it won't happen again.' I would never be able to forget what he had done. It was a warning sign – but a warning of what? I had no idea. I just wanted our life to go back to normal. Life resumed in our little yellow house with blue shutters, the backdrop to our life in retirement in the South of France. The pool cover was on. The oleanders had finished blooming. Autumn was drawing near.

In mid-October I had gone up to Paris, this time to look after the children of my son David, who was due to undergo minor surgery. I was always going back and forth whenever I was needed to look after one or another set of grandchildren. The school-holiday schedule became my own. I rushed up to Paris any time there was a problem too. I was Maminou, the travelling grandma. I wasn't afraid of getting old; I knew it was a privilege. Obviously when I was at David's I spent most of the time with my granddaughters. Every morning, Charlize stubbornly refused to wear anything but a tracksuit. Clémence, her twin sister, was always changing outfits and had a penchant for princess dresses. They were nine years old, the age I was when I lost my mother.

I didn't hear the phone ring that morning. I was sitting at the tennis courts. Clémence and I were watching Charlize as she ran after the ball. Her forehand had improved. I saw I had missed a call. Unknown number. I called back a little later. 'Bonjour, were you trying to reach me?' The man introduced himself: 'This is Deputy Sergeant Perret from the Carpentras police. Are you aware that we interviewed your husband a few weeks ago? Do you have any idea what this is about?' Yes, I said, my husband had told me everything. My answer resounded inside me like a quiet victory: transparency and trust were at the heart of our long marriage. And, I added, I had lived with this man for fifty years and he had never yet let me down.

'When will you be back?'

'On October 21st. I can come and see you straight away.'

'No, no. We have too much work to do. Come with your husband on November 2nd.'

*

And so November 2nd arrived. Dominique had no reason to sob like Papa had when Maman died. 'Don't worry, it's only a formality,' I said to Dominique as we arrived at the police station, a low, unassuming, modern building, yellow like our house, the colour of Provence. We walked in, each masked up with one of those pale-blue rectangles that now covered every mouth on the planet. We had just reported to the reception desk when a man with a crew cut leaned over the balustrade on the first floor of the police station. It was Deputy Sergeant Perret.

'I'll see Monsieur Pelicot first, then Madame afterwards,' he called down. Dominique walked up the staircase in his ill-matching jacket without looking back. A short while later the police officer reappeared and motioned for me to follow him. I went briskly up the stairs, assuming that I would find Dominique in Perret's office. He wasn't there. The police officer indicated the chair opposite him, far enough away from his desk that I could take off my mask. I immediately apologised profusely for what my husband had done. The man across from me was tall and solidly built, with a strong face above his wide shoulders. He seemed to embody authority, and yet there was something gentle and cautious in the way he talked to me. He asked me to confirm my identity and the date and place of my birth: December 7th 1952 in Villingen, in Germany. Maiden name: Guillou. Parents' names: Yves Guillou and Jeanne Prot. He asked me how Dominique and I first met, and I told him it was at my mother's sister's house in July 1971. It was, I added, a genuine case of love at first sight. He wanted to know how I would describe my husband's character.

'He's kind, attentive. He's a lovely guy. That's why we're still together.'

He asked if we liked to entertain. I replied that we often had friends over. He asked me to describe a typical evening. I said we didn't really have a routine, we weren't that old yet. He asked me what time I went to bed, whether it was at the same time as my husband, whether I took a nap in the afternoon. I was a little taken aback by his questions.

'Are you into swinging?'

I didn't understand any more. I heard myself replying no, never, how ghastly, I heard myself spluttering that swinging was not something I would ever consider. That I couldn't imagine anyone else touching me. That, for me, there needs to be love with sex. He asked me if I thought I knew my husband well, and whether I trusted that he would never hide anything from me. I said yes.

'I am going to show you some photographs and videos that you are not going to like.'

I sensed something rising in his voice – not only embarrassment, but a curious mix of danger and protectiveness. He told me that Dominique had been taken into custody for aggravated rape and for administering toxic substances. I think I burst into tears. I moved towards his desk and put my mask back on. He picked up a photograph and held it out to me. A woman in a suspender belt lying on her side. A Black man behind her, penetrating her.

'That's you in the photograph.'

'No, that's not me.'

I got out my glasses; he got out another photograph. The same woman on her back, a tattooed man alongside her.

'That's you.'

'No.'

I did not recognise those men. Nor that woman. Her cheek was so floppy, her mouth so limp. She looked like a rag doll.

A third photograph. The man had kept his firefighter's sweater on.

I couldn't hear what the police officer was saying. Or rather, I could hear him but it had nothing to do with me. It was like the echo of a faraway voice. 'This is your bedroom. Aren't those your bedside lamps?'

So? That is not me lying lifeless on the bed. It's a photoshopped picture. Made by someone trying to hurt Dominique. Just last night while we were watching the news on television, there was a woman who had been intubated because of Covid, and he'd said how he would hate to see me like that.

The officer says a number. He tells me fifty-three men had come to my house to rape me. I ask for water. My mouth is paralysed. A psychologist comes into the office. A young woman. I don't need her. I am far away, even though we are in the same room. I am secure in my happiness, *our* happiness. Our fiftieth wedding anniversary is coming up, and the memory of how we met is still clear in my mind. His smile. His shy expression. His long, curly hair falling to his shoulders. His Breton sweater. He was going to love me. My brain shut down in Deputy Sergeant Perret's office.

TWO

It was July 1971. I had come to stay with my Aunt Andrée for a few days after she'd lost her husband. I wanted to be there for her as she had always been there for me. Almost as soon as I arrived she started telling me about a young man called Dominique she had recently employed. Now that my uncle had passed away, she and her son needed help keeping their small electrical business afloat. It was right next to their house, a company called Gagneux, a wooden-fronted workshop covered with billboards advertising all kinds of new electrical technology. Modernisation was moving full steam ahead in the French countryside. 'There's so much work to do,' my aunt often said.

I recognised in her the mute suffering of the local people, the obligation to keep pace with the changing times, but I also saw my mother's milky skin. My mother had died nine years earlier in our house, which was almost right next door. In my aunt's gestures and voice I spied similarities and echoes of her sister, her favourite sister, they'd been like twins, so close, thick as thieves. I had come back to the countryside of my childhood, to the turbid source of my melancholy and my joy. I listened to my aunt talking about this new employee, who was currently helping my cousin put in electrical installations in neighbouring farms. I would get to meet him, she promised; he tended to stick around after work. He sometimes even stayed for dinner. His red Citroën 2CV was parked in front of the house, on the road between Châtillon-sur-Indre and Azay-le-Ferron. Nothing bad was ever going to happen to me here.

To get a sense of this place, you have to imagine the chateaux dotted around the landscape, the sometimes sumptuous, sometimes crumbling old buildings that were visible from the road or the train, and seemed to open doors on to other centuries, other worlds. When we were little, our mother brought my brother and me to stay every summer. I spent my childhood running around the grounds of empty castles. I don't think I ever dreamed of being a princess, or made up stories about Prince Charming, even though the round towers and pointed roofs of the Château d'Azay-le-Ferron might have come straight out of a fairy tale. I knew where I came from: my brother and I were the grandchildren of Marie and Roger Prot, peasants from the hamlet of Le Châtelier. I walked with my grandmother behind the goats and the dog, I watched her making cheese in the cellar, pulling the scalding laundry from the tub, piling it into the wheelbarrow to go and rinse it with a paddle in the public washing place in the village. And I drank *miot*, a mixture of water, sugar and wine, in which we dunked pieces of bread when we helped out at the grape harvest with our horse.

Lying in my little bed in the morning, I heard the voice of my grandfather, a carpenter, offering coffee to the workers. I listened to the reassuring ballet of the adults around me, felt their presence, their roles, their love. On the long kitchen table, there was always a big four-pound loaf of bread cut into thick slices, a steaming pot of coffee, a bowl of fromage blanc, freshly picked peaches.

I think it is the memory of that table that I am holding on to as I set the breakfast table every evening; it is nestled inside me, like those extensions tucked underneath old wooden tables, ready to be pulled out to their full length for family celebrations. I would like to extend its promises into infinity. In my memory, the cockerel still crows. The sun creeps through the slats in the shutters.

This setting should have grown hazy and picturesque, a distant memory of holidays, but the twentieth century was seeing dramatic changes. World War Two was slowly receding into a profound silence. Young people were leaving the countryside for the city and the suburbs, just as Maman and some of her brothers and sisters already had. Land consolidation in the countryside would soon expand estates and wipe out small-holders, with their little fields full of hedgerows, thickets and rocky slopes where snakes hid. Soon, the baker's and butcher's vans would no longer come to the village, honking their horns before cutting the motor and opening up their back doors. All those rough linen sheets, washed with methylene blue and hung out to dry in the sun, would end up in flea markets. But in 1957, in a move that ran counter to the rest of the world, our family relocated back there. The course of life was reversed.

I was five years old, my brother six, around the age when

memories become fixed. Our parents rented an unheated house, originally an outbuilding of the chateau. We lived on the second floor in a suite of large rooms with high ceilings and huge chimneys. There was a kitchen at the back. No bathroom, just a jug and a basin filled with water that we heated in the winter and drew from the big tub left outside in the summer to warm up in the sun. We only had to cross the meadow to go and find Aunt Jeanne. Our grandparents were a few minutes away by foot. The house was at the end of the main road that led to the Château d'Azay-le-Ferron.

The groundskeeper knew us well – Michel, me and all our cousins. He would see us walking down the street, a few centimes tinkling in our pockets, stopping at Mother Tanchoux's little grocery shop and then emerging, mouths filled with toffees, or fingers sticky from packets of sherbet powder, before heading back to the estate. We were as happy playing among alleys of trees clipped into straight lines in the French style as we were running along nearby paths and through fields. We crossed borders and centuries without noticing, understood nothing about the divisions between men, or their wars, for which Papa – a professional soldier who was only ever briefly home on leave – was constantly setting off.

But we were able to distinguish between the 2CVs and 4CVs that belonged to the locals, and the Citroën DSs that belonged to the rich people who parked in front of the patisserie in Azay-le-Ferron, famous for its millefeuille and a cake shaped like a melon (from which it got its name, 'melon with almonds') that was served with crème anglaise. And we knew why our grandmother always wore mourning dress even though our grandfather was still alive. I was with her and Maman the day one of my uncles came to tell us that Micheline had died. His eyes were red, and his two little boys stood next to him clutching their pillows. Their sister had got burnt when their mother was heating up the alcohol she used to pluck chickens; the liquid had spilled on her and she didn't survive the journey to the hospital. My cousin Micheline was dead. She was one of us, a little girl with cropped brown hair. Not the cousin I played with the most – she was older, twelve – but she was family. The next day, my grandmother put on the black dress that she would wear for the rest of her life. And all around us, the trees, fields and chateaux would bear witness to how we knew to hold our tears in.

Most of all, we knew that Maman was very ill. Sometimes she went to hospital and was brought back, pale and thin, on a trolley pushed by the ambulance drivers. I was always afraid that she would fall off, that she would roll on to the ground and never make it back inside the house. One day, as we were walking to school, one of my cousins let slip the word 'cancer'; she was talking about someone else, but the word stuck, it sounded like a possible explanation, and also like a death sentence. Soon after, Grand-mère began cycling over to our house to take care of everything, to look after us all, especially Maman. I watched her arrive in her black dress every morning, and leave every evening. Maman never cried, or at least never in front of us. So I never did either. I once heard her scream. The slightest pressure caused her pain. The cancer had reached her bones. No one could touch her any more. I watched my grandmother unroll long bands of white cotton that she padded behind Maman's shoulders. Her pelvis was in a plaster cast. Her bed had been moved into the kitchen near the window so that she was never alone. There was the red Formica table next to it with the Telefunken radio sitting on top, and the smell of polish with which Hélène, the cleaner, gave a high shine to the copper pieces Papa brought back from Algeria, where he had been deployed.

These memories were still vivid when I returned to my aunt's house in the summer of 1971. Everything in me was trembling. I was unsteady on my feet. The past was pulling me in, with all its happiness and tragedy, as if my life had already been mapped out. And then Dominique walked into the kitchen. I'd been stung between the eyes by a wasp that day, the venom was circulating, my eyelids were so swollen I could barely see. I must have looked unrecognisable. He reminded me of the pop star Julien Clerc, with his shoulder-length curls and his striped sweater.

He stayed late at my aunt's house that evening, obviously putting off the moment he would have to go home to his parents in Châtillon-sur-Indre. He appeared very fond of my family, who offered him a warmth he seemed never to have encountered before. As if he were seeking some kind of reparation or affection. I was too.

I was nineteen that summer, and living in Paris with my father, brother and stepmother, working as a secretary at a printing press that produced bank cheques. To Dominique, I was a Parisienne, with everything that the countryside can project on to that word. In fact, we were just two kids who had been pushed into working at a very young age. And we had both spent our childhood scraping our knees in this corner of the Indre. His shyness reassured me. He blushed a lot. He was not one of those self-assured young men. I knew nothing of love, I had never even had a flirtation, but I just knew that he was going to love me. The fact that I met him at Andrée's house was a sign, a sign from Maman that she was watching over me. This man was going to fall in love with me. And my life, which had lost its meaning, was about to take on a new purpose.

As soon as I got back to Paris, I told my father about him. He poured cold water on my enthusiasm. He said that I was too young, that we had no life experience. As a career soldier, he disapproved of the fact that Dominique had avoided military service. I think he didn't want to let me go. I was not yet legally an adult, but I was earning my living, and every weekend I would take the train to the Indre to be with Dominique, bringing him gifts of sweaters and cologne I had bought in Paris. I was drawing him towards me, towards the city and away from his family, whom I was only beginning to get to know. His mother, Juliette, said that he would be unhappy in Paris. She was fifty, and already looked worn out by life. His father, Denis Pelicot, seemed to be constantly shouting. They often spoke admiringly of his brother, Joël, who was studying medicine in Tours, whereas Dominique had left school early and still handed over his electrician's salary to his parents each month. He shared a bedroom with Nicole, a little girl with a learning disability who was a ward of the state being fostered by the family. The other bedroom was where his paternal grandfather slept. For many years he had been a porter at a grand hotel in Trouville, and from the way they said it, it was as if he had returned from a distant continent. He suffered from Parkinson's now. Dominique's parents slept in the living room. I sensed how bleak their world was, their sad lives behind all those closed doors.

And yet it was under that very roof that we made love for the first time. I kept putting the moment off, I wanted to be sure, I needed to know he was the One. He was in more of a hurry, but was prepared to wait until I was ready. It happened one night in May 1972. I was visiting for the weekend, staying at his parents' house, and since we weren't married, I had been given his grandfather's room. In the middle of the night Dominique sneaked in. It was my first time, and his too. I remember the softness of skin on skin, how shy we were, and obviously a little awkward. Afterwards he slipped back to his own room, leaving me with the impression that we had made a pact. We were lovers and we were twins. We would always be together; our suffering behind us, we would escape from our damaged families. I would be his cure and he would be mine. A few months later he came up to Paris to ask my father for my hand in marriage. My father didn't dare say no.

'For better or for worse,' declared the man who married us on April 14th 1973. I became Gisèle Pelicot. The celebration was a simple one. We had no money. Dominique wore a carnation in his buttonhole. There is a beautiful wedding photograph of the two of us, taken in the castle grounds, in the shadow of the Château d'Azay-le-Ferron.

I was starting a new life. I was in love.

THREE

I wanted to go home.

'Will you be pressing charges?' Deputy Sergeant Perret asked.

'Yes.' The word came out of my mouth sounding so meek. If he hadn't asked the question, it never would have occurred to me. I just wanted this to stop. To go home. To get back to my normal life. I signed the crime report form he held out to me, as if signing a disclaimer. Then my statement. I scribbled PCT, the abbreviation of Pelicot, at the bottom of each page, without reading any of it, without seeing that I had also said yes: 'Yes, that is me, that's my room.' Those are the words that are written on the document; those are the words the police heard me say. It's all so different from what I remember. My head was screaming no – no, it's not me, it's not him. 'I don't know where I am any more.' Those words are written too. That's what I said.

Laurent Perret suggested a colleague take me home. 'You should call someone, you mustn't be alone,' he said. When I finally left the police station, Dominique must have still been there. A police officer drove my car and parked in the gravel driveway in front of the garage. He did not come inside. He left immediately in the police vehicle that had followed us to the house. I opened the front door with relief, as if coming home might erase the hours that had just passed – as if I could forget them, as I had forgotten so many things over the last few years. I'd forgotten what we'd done for my birthday only a day before. I'd forgotten saying goodbye to the children when they left. I'd forgotten I'd been to the hairdresser, even though I could see in the mirror that my hair had just been cut and coloured. I had been having more and more of these memory lapses. I dreaded them. I was afraid to drive, I was afraid to take the train, I was afraid I'd miss my station. I was afraid I was dying. But that day, I deliberately wanted to summon that emptiness into my head. I wanted to forget that I had just come home from the police station, alone.

Impossible. While we were at the station, investigators had been to the house to carry out a search. They'd turned the whole place upside down. I started tidying up. Everything had to be back in its place. I put a load of laundry in the washing machine. Then I rang Pierre, my son-in-law, and left a message: 'Pierre, can you call me back? It's about Dominique.' That was it. No details. Telling and not telling. I had no idea what I was going to say to the children. I vacuumed the living room. I called my friend Sylvie: 'Can you come over? I have to talk to you.' No explanation, like my message to Pierre. She said she would come right away. I was still reeling. I hung Dominique's boxer shorts, pyjamas and trousers on the washing line in the garden. It was a sunny day, the clothes would dry in no time. Everything was nice and clean. I was like a dog waiting by the garden gate for its master. He'd be back soon. His car was in the garage. I vacuumed the bedrooms and started on the pile of ironing.

Sylvie arrived. 'Are you ill?' She was afraid I had Covid. We sat down.

'Dominique's been arrested. He raped me. He brought people to the house to rape me, for years.'

I managed to find a way to say the thing that my whole being refused to hear, the thing that all the obsessive cleaning and tidying I had been doing for the last two hours had been an attempt to block out, as I begged the washing machine, the vacuum cleaner, the iron to give me back my life. A wave of shame swelled up inside me as I read the incredulity on Sylvie's face. She knew Dominique well, she'd known him for years. We had met at work originally; she was a reserved young woman in the resource management department at EDF, the French national electricity supplier. We'd struck up a friendship and began socialising as couples outside the office. She and her husband used to so enjoy staying with us during the summer that they decided to retire to Mazan too. She didn't understand. Her state of shock confirmed mine: it wasn't possible. But when the police officer called to check that someone was with me, that I wasn't alone, there was so much concern for me in his voice that it made me realise the weight and significance of the case file he was putting together.

'Can you look to see if you can find any medication in the house? We couldn't find any,' he said.

So that was what they had been looking for while we were at the police station. What it takes to change a woman into a dead weight, her features melted on to the pillow so that she doesn't even have a face any more.

Pierre finally called early in the afternoon. He was also worried I might have Covid. That morning he had left a cheerful message for his father-in-law: the itinerary of the Tour de France had just been announced, and the ascent of Mont Ventoux would take place when they were staying with us in Mazan, what good news! And here I was, once again forced to say what I didn't want to hear.

'Your father-in-law's been arrested. He raped me and he had me raped by others.'

Pierre didn't say anything. I went on. I needed his help. I didn't know how to tell Caroline about what was happening. Of all my children, my daughter is the least predictable. She's one of those highly strung people who love and lose their temper in the same breath. She seems to have been filled since childhood with a feeling of insecurity that I have never really understood or been able to soothe. She was forty-one. I was afraid of telling her, afraid of how she would react. She was about to go through hell and back, that much I knew. I was worried about her. Pierre, who lived with her, understood. He said he'd let me know the minute she got home.

Deputy Sergeant Perret came to the house. He was relieved to see Sylvie. He wanted another strand of my hair – the sample taken that morning was insufficient. I let him take some of the fine hairs from the back of my neck. Later I learned they are traps for chemical substances and can reveal poisoning. The laundry hanging in the garden was already dry. Dominique's boxer shorts and trousers dangling over a void. How I loved our garden and the single-storey house we had chosen for our old age. I pictured him a few weeks earlier, sitting on our leather sofa and weeping, saying he couldn't bear to lose me. Suddenly I realised he must have already known what was awaiting him; he knew what he was dragging us into, because his computer and his phone had already been seized by the police. And there I was imagining I was seeing the mirror image of my father's grief.

It gets dark early in November. I locked up and then drove behind Sylvie to her house. Her husband, Michel, had got out a bottle of champagne. Sylvie must have warned him before our arrival, and I imagined him trying to figure out what he could do or say, then putting the champagne in the fridge to blur the line between good times and bad. I drained my glass, grateful for the small gesture of positivity. Caroline called around seven o'clock. I didn't answer. I didn't want her to be alone when I told her. I sent another message to Pierre. He texted back that he would let me know as soon as she got home. 'You have to stay right by her side,' I insisted.

A short while later he messaged to say that she was outside parking the car. I waited five minutes before I called. 'Is Pierre with you? I think you should sit down.' I told her that her father was in custody. That he had drugged me and raped me. Brought other men to the house to rape me. She began to scream. A shriek of anguish. The howl of a wounded animal. My daughter was breaking down. The words I was saying to try and calm her were not getting through. Pierre took the phone from her, said a couple of words to me, and hung up.

Then I called David, my elder son. 'Sit down. I have bad

news,' I said softly. I could hear my voice. I was talking like a robot. He listened without reacting. Everyone knows there will be difficult things we have to tell our children, but not this, nothing like this, this is beyond the boundaries of what can be imagined. Sure, things can fall apart, but not like this.

David didn't respond. Eventually he said, 'I have to go, Maman.' Later I found out he had run to the toilet to vomit.

Florian, our youngest, was calm and composed when we spoke. He asked how I was and where I was. I told him I was spending the night at Sylvie's, I wasn't alone, I was going to sleep in the guest room upstairs.

I didn't sleep a wink that night. Almost every fifteen minutes one or other of the children rang, terrified I was falling apart, just as their own childhoods were collapsing. They kept calling me, and then each other, to discuss and pick apart the last few years. It was Caroline who said, in the middle of the night, 'But Maman, all those memory lapses, it has to be that!'

I hadn't made the connection, despite what the police officer had told me, the house search and the two samples of hair. Dominique had always been there to witness my memory losses. He was the one who reassured me and took me to the doctor; he was the one to whom my hairdresser had confided her concerns that time I'd completely forgotten I'd been in for an appointment. I went back the next day to try to piece together what had happened. She told me how relieved she was when I walked in again, and described my blank expression in the mirror the day before, my mechanical responses to her questions, how she had been afraid I might be having a stroke, how she'd suggested to Dominique I get some tests done as a matter of urgency. He was my ally.

I had become convinced I was going to die like my mother. It was my destiny; I had a brain tumour. A brain scan in 2017 proved me wrong, but that wasn't enough to banish the idea from my head. The doctors assured me it was just anxiety, but that didn't make sense to me: one morning, like Maman, I was not going to wake up. My whole existence revolved around this tragedy. I had wanted my life to be a redemption, but it turned out it was simply a continuation. It was genetic. I felt it. I let myself be taken in by this scenario as the memory lapses became more and more frequent. Even my children had witnessed them. There was one occasion they told me about later, when I was on the phone to my grandson Maxime, Caroline and Pierre's son, and I kept repeating the same thing over and over like a broken record. The little boy was so embarrassed that his parents motioned to him to hang up. A neurologist friend of Pierre's said she thought it might be Alzheimer's. David's wife, Céline, murmured that they ought to think about putting me in a home. The signs were alarming. When the children called it was not unusual for their father to tell them I was too tired to speak. Whenever they came to visit, though, I was fine, there was never anything wrong, except for one time when everyone was leaving to go back to Paris. I had spent lunch slumped in my chair, my arm falling continually as if I couldn't control it. Florian was clearly upset, he didn't want to leave, but his father frogmarched him to the car and said, 'Don't worry, she's just tired, I'm going to put her to bed.'

He was going to put me to bed, yes. To rape me and invite other men to rape me a few hours after my son had left. He knew that the poison in my wine glass or on my plate was taking effect.

But that first night I didn't try to piece together all the various events, it was too soon. Too painful. The children worked it out more quickly. They bought themselves train tickets to Avignon. 'We'll be there tomorrow,' they announced in the middle of the night.

The next morning, I left Sylvie's and went back to the house, drawn by the urge to be in my own home and to salvage a few good memories and strength from it. The first thing I saw was that the police were back. 'Where are the walking boots kept?' one of the investigators asked. I showed him a shelf in the garage. He pulled a pair of socks folded into a ball from one of the boots and unrolled it. Out fell some blister packs of pills. Open. Sealed. Mostly lorazepam, an anxiety and insomnia medication. Dominique had clearly ended up talking.

Suddenly my house was no longer my home. It was full of shadows, hiding places, nooks and crannies and poison. And where was all the sexy underwear the sleeping woman wore? Not in my chest of drawers, that was for sure. My pants and bras are white and maroon. Those are the colours I like. I always bought them myself. It's true that sometimes Dominique would point things out in lingerie displays: 'Look, they're pretty,' he'd say. I never paid any attention. That kind of thing wasn't me at all.

But there was that one time in Printemps, the department store on Place de la Nation in Paris. I was hesitating between two sets, we couldn't afford both. While I was paying for the set I had chosen, Dominique slipped the other into his pocket, but he was stopped by security and made to pay for it before he could leave. 'Madame, you mustn't be cross with your husband,' the sales assistant entreated. 'It's such a sweet thing to do.' What to do with these memories?

I drove back to the police station, where the children and I had arranged to meet. They were on their way in a taxi from Avignon station. The fleeting temptation to let go of the steering wheel and put an end to everything crossed my mind – no more than a few seconds, the time it took to dismiss it. I would never give death a helping hand.

When David, Caroline and Florian arrived, I must have looked exhausted and vulnerable, completely lost in my big down coat. One after the other they took me in their arms. I clung to them as tightly as they clung to me. It was so good to feel their presence. I was completely rigid, desperate not to let myself go. I didn't want to break down and cry. Alone, yes, but not in front of them. After we'd embraced, we all went inside. Deputy Sergeant Perret waved them into a small office on the ground floor while I waited alone at reception. I didn't know what they were talking about – I just hoped they wouldn't see the photographs. When they came out, Perret called me back in to see me again.

'Why didn't you tell me about your health concerns and your memory loss?' he asked.

It was Caroline who had brought this up. Perret had told

them about the pills they had found at the house, and shown them prescriptions from our family doctor that had also been seized. The doctor had been prescribing lorazepam, Viagra and zolpidem to my husband, who must have been complaining about having trouble sleeping and getting an erection because of stress over our financial problems. I told Perret the truth: I hadn't made the connection. Yes, I was concerned, yes, I had become a shadow of myself. I was forgetting so much. I had even booked an appointment for an MRI, because I wasn't satisfied with the brain scan. Should I tell him that I was certain I was going to die of a brain tumour like my mother, that the black hole of my childhood sucked everything into it, extinguishing any question, suspicion or grievance? Should I admit that I was so sure of it that sometimes I said to myself, if this is what it is to die, it's okay, it's not so painful, and that this was how I reconciled myself to death, my mother's and my own? What was the point? The thread of my thoughts led too far back in time, too far from his investigations. It led to a place where I had to go alone.

The children and I went back to the house together. I remember thinking with relief that there was some leftover pumpkin soup in the fridge for dinner. All they were thinking about was going through drawers and cupboards. Searching. Discovering things they had never suspected. Florian began with his father's desk. He found a speeding ticket given at two in the morning. What was he doing driving in the middle of the night? They all stared at me as if I had an answer. Their parents had turned into a pair of strangers. The phone rang.

It was the police officer. He wanted to see the children again. Caroline and Florian went down to the station where Perret showed them two photographs of a young woman asleep, found on their father's computer. 'Is this you?' he asked Caroline. It was.

She was in a dreadful, almost crazed state when she got back. Had he done something to her too? This was the first I had heard of these photos, and I would only see them later when the case file was being compiled. Now the main thing was to assuage her fears, but what could we say to reassure her after such a horrifying discovery? Her suspicions were mounting, and her brothers' too. It was all going too fast for me.

Night fell. As I headed for my bedroom, Caroline suggested I come and sleep with her, away from that now cursed place where everything had happened. But I had a visceral need to be alone. It's hard to deny your child that, but if I had joined her, if I had allowed my pain to swell with hers, I'd have collapsed and ended up an additional burden on my children. I was sure of it, it was my survival instinct that guided me. I needed time and silence to digest everything I had just found out. I needed to find my strength. She, on the other hand, did not want to be on her own. She asked her brother to come and sleep in her room. Florian moved his mattress next to her bed. And I lay down in my own bed. The scene of rape, but still my bed.

Would it have made things easier if I had snuggled up to my daughter, if we had stayed up all night talking? I don't know. The next morning I was up early. She came into the kitchen, restless and jittery. I felt incredibly sad. I was like a robot, clinging to the next task, the next hour. We started going over the events of the last couple of days. Though I understood her suspicions – from now on, nothing about this horror could be ruled out – I couldn't let them become certainties. But to her my words sounded like denial. I tried to reassure her. I told her that we needed to give the judicial police time to establish the facts, time to search through her father's computer files. But we were so different in our approaches to life and its tragedies. This was not the first tragedy I had experienced. I was familiar with the suit of armour I had to don to face the world. I was not going to let myself drown as my father and brother had, and I wanted to help Caroline stay afloat too.

We got going on the huge task of sorting out the house. The children instructed me to gather up what I wanted to take with me, since we were leaving for Paris the next day. Suddenly Caroline yanked open the doors of the sideboard and began grabbing plates, sending them flying across the room one after another and yelling that I didn't need them any more.

'Caroline, don't break everything, please, there are things I'd like to keep.'

'What can you possibly want to keep from that life?' she cried.

Everything was splintering. Objects. Our history. Us. Me, a little more with each passing moment. Caroline ran into the corridor and tore down a picture her father had painted, a nude woman seen from behind. She had always said she wanted to inherit it after he died. Now she went out on to the terrace and started trying to rip it to pieces. As she attacked it the title appeared, written in pencil on the back of the canvas, utterly terrifying in light of what we had learned: *Coercion*. Eventually she managed to destroy it completely. Then she started on the framed photographs that hung throughout the house, and the photo albums stored in a trunk. All our holidays and Christmases, our youth, their childhood – she ripped up the lot. Page after page. Her brothers didn't try to stop her. They carried on calmly combing through their father's desk. But they undoubtedly shared their sister's rage; all their memories had suddenly turned out to be unbearable lies. But mine hadn't. I clung to my memories, I wanted to hold on to those pictures of a father, a husband, a family built by two messed-up kids from the Indre who got married in the shadow of a beautiful chateau. Of course our children could not tell themselves the same story, so I left them to it, a stranger in my own home. All I managed to do was keep our inquisitive neighbour at bay. She'd been alerted by all the screaming and crashing and I caught her poking her head over the fence into the courtyard. 'You're not at the circus, you know,' I snapped.

The house was wrecked by sorrow. David and Florian piled the debris into rubbish bags and loaded them into their father's car. When it was full, they left for the dump; when they came back, they loaded up the car again. They made several trips and soon it was not just debris they were carting away, but the wicker garden chairs, and most of their father's clothes and belongings too.

Caroline was in a bad way the next day. She called a psychologist recommended to her by a friend. I watched through the window as she talked, pacing up and down the terrace where we ate in the summer. She told the psychologist what we had just found out, and described the two photographs of her asleep. I only caught snatches of the conversation. Eventually Caroline hung up and stormed back into the house like a fury.

'He's killed me! He's killed me!' she screamed.

The psychologist, who had never met her and was speaking to her for the first time, had hinted that it was very likely she had been raped by her father. She fell to the floor. Florian moved her into the recovery position, while I ran to get her a glass of sugary water. We called the emergency services, who said we should take her straight to the hospital, but Florian and David didn't want us to miss our train that afternoon, they couldn't bear to spend another night in the house. They found a doctor in Mazan who prescribed Caroline a tranquilliser.

It was time to leave. I didn't want to. I wanted to spend the day at home and sleep at Sylvie's. I wanted to keep walking around the house. But I didn't protest. I didn't have the strength to say no to them. They talked to me as if they were speaking to a child. I obeyed. They meant well. They thought it was their duty to look after me. I followed them.

Sylvie dropped us at the station. All I had with me were two suitcases and Lancôme, our little bulldog, on his leash, still waiting for his master's return. We sped away on the high-speed train. There were long silences between us, a mixture of exhaustion and shock. I was slowly beginning to put two and two together, but mostly I had the peculiar feeling of being inside an enormous shredder. My children had lives to go back to. I had nothing.

Arriving at the Gare de Lyon in Paris was in a way the most painful moment of all. It still makes me cry to think about it. I had no idea what I was doing there. The crowd on the platform was like a swarm of flies bearing down on me. The void was sucking me in. It was the old fault line beneath my feet; it had been there all along and now it was opening up again, swallowing everything that I held dear.

FOUR

I was born in Villingen, a small town in West Germany, in 1952. It's hard to summon up any memories of the place, I was so little when we left. It's also hard to ignore the fact that I was born in a country in ruins, the very reason we were there. After the war, Germany had been stripped of its sovereignty and carved up by the Allies into four zones, one of which was occupied by the French. My father, Yves, had followed his regiment, and my mother, Jeanne, had followed her young husband.

I have only one photograph of them from that time. They are standing in a meadow in the countryside, a lake just visible in the background, their arms around each other, very close, obviously in love. The catastrophe is behind them. They seem all alone in the world, happy to be living in this defeated Germany that had ravaged their youth. My father has the toned, muscular body of a soldier and my mother's waist swells beneath a loose blouse. She must be expecting my brother, Michel.

I was born the following December. My father insisted I be called Gisèle, the name his mother would have given a daughter if she'd had one. He held tight to the few precious memories he had of her. She died of tuberculosis when he was seven. Is that where the taint of misfortune began? Was my birth supposed to erase it?

Another photograph. My father as a young man in uniform. He must be about seventeen. He looks like a kid. His hair is slicked back and he sports a little cap on the side of his head, like the American soldiers who peopled his teenage years. He has joined up. At some point later he jotted down on the back of the photo: 'December 1945. My first leave. Papa.' He must have gone home for a few days to see his family in Scaër, in Brittany. The town still bore the scars of the terrible battles of August 1944, when the Resistance rose up against the Nazi occupiers in the wake of the D-Day landings in Normandy. Our surname, Guillou, is carved on the war memorial, a lad named Corentin who was executed by the Nazis at the age of twenty-one. I don't know whether he was a member of our extended family – we were never told anything about him if he was – but the blood that flowed at the Liberation certainly marked my father's adolescence and forged his ambition to become a soldier. It was better than going off to work at the factory like his two brothers, and their father before them. His father had remarried, and then his second wife died in childbirth, leaving him with two motherless infants to care for. More misfortune. The infernal noise of the machines and huge rolls of paper from the Cascadec paper mill that you could hear from inside the house, all the way up the hill, was sucking my father in. It was his turn. But my father preferred looking out to sea, towards the open horizon and liberating winds. He wanted to join the navy, but he was turned down for being too short, so he joined the army instead. It was at a navy dance that he met my mother a few years later. That was how he always put it – 'at a navy dance on the banks of the Seine' – without ever explaining how they had both ended up on the dance floor in Paris that night. She had come to the city all the way from the Berry region in central France, he from the Brittany coast.

Another photograph, taken in Paris, the two of them decked out in their Sunday best. It's one of the ones my cousin gave me recently. I handle them with great care. They are the only traces of my parents together that I possess. Sometimes I think that without photographs, memories wouldn't exist, at least not in enough detail to make recollections come alive. My father must have sent this one to his family in Brittany. He's wearing civilian clothes, a belted trench coat with epaulettes. My mother is in a white fitted suit, with a rigid handbag hanging from her wrist. She looks happy and confident. And her smile – ah, that smile! My Aunt Andrée used to tell me she was always smiling. That smile is my inheritance. And, I think, my father's shield. He is looking away from the camera, almost as if he were trying to evade it. And when I peer more closely at this photo taken on a Parisian street, I see that everyone – even the gawkers in the background – is looking at the person taking the picture, except my father. Was he on leave? Had he already been deployed to Indochina? People say that those who have been to war cannot bear the nonchalance of crowds when they come back. There's no date on the photograph. Difficult to say. Perhaps my father's elusive expression lasted no more than an instant. Or it was a veil of anxiety that never left him. A young couple about to get married, or just married, who were soon to move to Germany.

I have three photographs of us in Germany. A modern interior, two young parents, each with a baby in their lap, Maman in a long negligée. These pictures conjure up my earliest sensations of the cold German winter, the cosy cable-knit sweaters my mother made for us, the delicious Bratwurst sausages we ate in the street and the beauty of the Christmas market. We lived in Reutlingen, a garrison town, whose long grey buildings housed the French artillery and cavalry. History's open wounds and bitterness were all around us, visible still in the stationary tanks and training grounds where we risked falling into ditches as we leapt over them. But as far back as I can remember, the thing that most fascinated me was the serving hatch in the kitchen. You lifted the flap, slid the plate in and took it out in the dining room on the other side. It was like a little hiding place. I used to put my toys in there, anything that fell into my hands. I was tempted to make myself tiny and go through the wall. It was like a secret passage.

The memory of what happened next cancels out everything. This I can recall in detail. I am four and a half, the pavement is icy, Maman slips and falls on the way to school. She manages to get up, slowly, but a friend insists on taking her to the doctor after she has dropped us off. Michel goes to his classroom, but I refuse. I won't let go of her hand, I want to stay with her, I don't know why but suddenly I am afraid for her. That's how I find myself standing next to her under a doctor's huge, blinding light, how I see the circle of red, burnt skin under her long hair, hidden at the back of her skull where her hair hasn't grown back. The wound scares me, and even more so what it conceals, everything I am not being told.

Maman was living on borrowed time.

Two years earlier Papa had felt a lump as he ran his fingers through her hair. The tumour was treated with radiation that burnt her without offering much hope. The doctor could not promise she had more than six months to live. A battle began, a fight to the death. That explains why Papa was always leaving, why he went on more and more missions. He went away to earn more money so he could pay for the best doctors and the best treatment available. He was desperate to extend her reprieve, maybe some days he even believed he could save her. They would escape. He refused to let history repeat itself, to see the same tragedy play out, to lose his wife after he'd lost his mother, to see his children motherless as he had been. A year went by, then two. A victory: Maman was still alive. But Papa was never at home to enjoy being with her, and we could never enjoy being with the two of them, apart from during his brief periods of leave.

It was not long after her fall and my discovery of what lay under her hair that we moved to Azay-le-Ferron. I don't know if this return to Maman's birthplace indicated that she was near the end. She went home to be close to her parents and her brothers and sisters. My father needed their help. He was always leaving and coming back. Another year went by, then another. Maman was wasting away. I was growing up. I watched over her.

I am reminded of Maman slipping oranges into her blouse to make us laugh. Her breasts have entirely wasted away. It is her last summer. One day she asks me to post a letter for her. She is worried. There has been a plane crash in Rabat and she is afraid for my father. Off I go, giving her a big smile. I run all the way to the post office, hurry up, Mr Postman, this is a letter to my father from my dying mother who is afraid he might already be dead.

A few months later Maman breaks it to me gently that Santa Claus is coming to take her away. I thought he would make her better, protect her, heal her. Even bring her back to us. Santa Claus brings presents, doesn't he? I still believe in him even though I am nearly nine.

Christmas and New Year come and go. It is 1962. Papa is still at home; this time his leave seems to be lasting much longer than usual.

It is the very end of January. One Wednesday evening Michel and I are watching *La Piste aux étoiles*, a hugely popular television show about the circus. We are completely entranced by the music, the orchestra, the elephants, the acrobats and clowns bursting out from behind the heavy curtain. We were among the first people in the village to get a television. Papa is watching with us. His leave really is lasting for a long time. We are sitting in the bedroom because Maman's bed is in the kitchen now. Grand-mère comes in to tell Papa she has put a hot-water bottle on Maman's feet because they are so cold, she hasn't moved, maybe he should go and take a look at her. I am on my feet as soon as he stands up from his armchair. Something compels me to follow him into the kitchen. Papa leans over Maman. He closes her eyelids. 'Nanou,' he whispers. I hear the most terrible grief and fear well up in his voice, as if he is calling to her, while I gently shake her shoulder to wake her up.

That night, I was sent to sleep at my Aunt Jeanne's, the wife of my mother's older brother. She had the same name as Maman, and she was just as kind. Michel went to Aunt Andrée's house, because her son was almost the same age as him. We were separated that night and for several days afterwards. When we were allowed to come home, Maman was still in her bed, dressed in her nice striped jacket and skirt with her hair in a long plait over her left shoulder, and her hands crossed. I thought she was still asleep.

My father didn't want us to go to the funeral. He didn't want us to watch her coffin go down into the ground, or to see him collapse, as he did when he was leaving the cemetery. A perforated ulcer burst in his chest. I saw him cry later, sitting in my aunt's kitchen. He kept saying how unfair it was. That he was the soldier, the one ready to die at war, not her, she could have lived off his war pension. He did take us to the cemetery one day. It was snowing. I remember at the graveside thinking she couldn't possibly be comfortable there.

For a long time afterwards I was afraid to fall asleep. Afraid of the night from which I might never wake up. It was as if I were dissolving into my mother's body, as if I were still seeking answers: Where was she? When was she coming back? For several months after her death I lived with Aunt Jeanne and my brother with Aunt Andrée. We didn't even see each other at school; he was at the boys' school, and I was at the girls'. At last, in mid-July, my father came to take us home. Sometimes he got angry for no reason, and the long lock of hair he combed towards the back of his head would tumble over his face. As far as I knew only Maman's death could explain these dark moments. The Algerian war had just ended. He never mentioned it to us. He must have talked about it to other people. He got a job at the War Ministry. We moved to Paris.

We lived for a short while with my mother's brother Claude and his wife, Paulette, in rue de l'Yvette, near the Jasmin metro station. Claude was a roofer and went off to work on his moped. One day I saw Henri Salvador drive by in a pink Cadillac. Eventually Papa found us an apartment to rent at 218 bis, Avenue Daumesnil, in the 12th arrondissement. What was wonderful was that the neighbourhood was full of Maman's relatives. There was her godmother Marthe, who had a hairdressing salon on the avenue. And her youngest brother, who lived at 55 rue de Fécamp, where his wife, Louisette, was the concierge. They had a little caretaker's apartment that had a toilet outside in the courtyard and was heated with coal that they went to fetch in a scuttle from the local café. Their son Philippe was a bit younger than us, but we all went back together to his house for lunch because Papa didn't want us to eat in the school canteen, and in the evenings after school we would retrace our steps and stay at Aunt Louisette's until he came to collect us.

We formed a trio, grandchildren of peasants who had become Parisians. Avenue Daumesnil was our stomping ground. At the very end of the avenue was the Museum of the Colonies, its imposing facade adorned with sculptures of exotic characters. Further still was the Bois de Vincennes and the lake, the outer limit of our wanderings. I always said bonjour to every single person I passed on the street, just as I had in Azay-le-Ferron. I didn't want to upset anyone. Adults seemed unable to do otherwise.

Papa was sad. Marthe, my mother's godmother whose hairdressing salon I loved to visit, sighed when I told her I wanted to be a hairdresser like her when I grew up. 'Choose something else,' she said. 'It's absolutely exhausting, you're on your feet all day, and handling all these poisonous dyes.' Meanwhile, whenever Aunt Louisette decided my hair needed tidying up, she would grab the brush and push it against my head and tug my hair so hard, it was as if she had a grudge against the entire world. It hurt, but I never said anything, I didn't complain, I didn't care. It wasn't how my mother brushed my hair. That was something I would never feel again, it was gentle and protective, and I thought about it often.

At school, when we were supposed to make a card for Mother's Day, the teacher said, 'Just make one for your father instead.' Three years later he got married again. His new wife was a widow called Marie-Joséphine, who lived on the first floor of her family house in Brittany. Her older brother, Jo, had set them up when we were there on holiday. And just like with Maman's funeral, my father didn't want us at the wedding. They came to pick us up from school after the ceremony. Her daughter was with them. I watched them from the safe distance of a window in the corridor. I didn't want to go home, I didn't want anyone to replace Maman. Papa had not chosen a substitute mother for us; Marie-Joséphine was Maman's polar opposite. She had such thin, pursed lips it looked like she had a minus sign above her jaw. Not a single kind word ever escaped them. I don't think my father was trying to find love again. His greatest, craziest, most beautiful love story had ended with my mother's death. He was simply bringing another female presence into our lives. It reassured him.

We carried on living in the same neighbourhood, but moved to a small apartment complex of modern grey buildings at 44 bis, rue de la Vega. Our building was eight storeys high, and we lived on the sixth. Our stepmother declared that from now on we would eat in the school canteen, she had no desire to have us home for lunch every day. She hid the coffee and the butter. She hid apples inside the washing machine. Dessert was always yoghurt or fruit. Her obsession with saving money was a poor disguise for the hardships she inflicted on us. She switched off the hot water when I was in the middle of washing my hair, claiming I took too long to rinse it and was wasting water. Behind her back I called her Folcoche, after the cruel mother in Hervé Bazin's novel *Viper in the Fist*. I could see that Michel was suffering too.

We were always running off to play with our cousin Philippe. Now we began venturing further afield. There was a grotto on one of the two little islands in the middle of the lake in the Bois de Vincennes where we acted out adventures. There was nothing remotely untamed about it, with its landscaped waterfront – it even had a white-columned rotunda on top – but we loved crouching on the mossy rocks inside the damp cave. For a few hours we were no longer pawns in the bitter games played by adults or in the school playground. One day I came out of the grotto and decided to go for a paddle. I stepped into the water fully dressed and immediately started to sink, sucked down by the sludge. The lake was slowly submerging me. I was on my back going under. I don't remember struggling. My body rose to the surface, then sank back into the muddy water, and I didn't react. I let myself go. Was that what dying was like? Then a man's hand hauled me out of the water. Michel and Philippe had called for help. I had not.

I was twelve the year our father remarried. My body was changing; puberty was sketching out its new contours. Papa, I found out later, had discreetly asked my Aunt Louisette to prepare me for what was in store. She took me aside and told me not to be scared, one day I would find blood in my underpants, but I mustn't worry about it. My father could never have asked my stepmother to talk about such feminine intimacies, she would have been utterly incapable. All she ever told me was that I was fat and looked like a carthorse, not like her beautiful daughter, she was like a racehorse. I remember that equine comparison. Words have more power to hurt at that age than any other, and childhood shame is not soon forgotten. Perhaps it was this new body of mine that I was abandoning to the mercy of the lake and of oblivion.

But who would protect Maman's smile? Who would keep it alive, unless I did? My brother was crushed by sadness. He was no longer the bright, lively little boy I used to roam around the countryside with. His chubby body seemed swollen with bitter tears. My stepmother was particularly harsh with him. He was falling behind at school. The day of his First Communion he looked completely browbeaten. Our father, the soldier, had wanted a grand luncheon with all the uncles and aunts at the officers' mess at the Ecole Militaire in Paris, for the pomp of the army to cover our hardship. 'God helps those who help themselves!' he always liked to say. But he seemed just as despairing as his son. The events of the previous few years had left a deep, enduring melancholy in my father's eyes.

I still sucked my thumb at night. During the day I contemplated what my purpose in life might be. As soon as I turned fourteen, I started looking for work during the school holidays. Michel came along with me, and we presented ourselves at a factory in Ménilmontant. The job was assembling the casings of telephones. I was hired, but my brother wasn't. He was offered a job in a workshop making funeral wreaths. We left the house together in the morning and came home together at night. During the day I had little springs at my fingertips, while he had graveyard ornaments.

The further he drifted, the tougher I became. I was a steadfast tin soldier of joy. With my first wages, I bought a dressing gown for my father for Christmas, and a powder compact for my stepmother. She barely glanced at it. 'She'd do better to save her money,' she tutted, loud enough for me to hear. I didn't understand.

I spent my free time now with Françoise, my best friend from school. We sensed that times were changing, but we weren't entirely sure how this concerned us. We listened out for the sounds and the names of central Paris; we talked about famous couples like Simone de Beauvoir and Jean-Paul Sartre, Louis Aragon and Elsa Triolet; we'd heard of *The Second Sex* though it never occurred to us to read it. The Café de Flore, a few metro stops from where we lived, might as well have been a distant planet. We preferred going to the Louvre, for its vast galleries, the creaking parquet floors, the smell of wax. I liked to drag Françoise to look at *The Coronation of Napoleon* by Jacques-Louis David. I told her about how the emperor's mother hadn't been present at the ceremony in Notre-Dame, but Napoleon had asked the artist to include her in the painting. I think that was why I liked the picture so much, because it inserted the mother where she wasn't. Françoise must have found me very imaginative, because she was convinced I was going to be a writer like Colette.

I was sixteen when I was first offered the opportunity to travel abroad. I had taken over as the nanny for a wealthy family who lived on Boulevard du Général Koenig, in Neuilly-sur-Seine. The mother was French, the father American, with hair like President Kennedy. I looked after their four little girls over the Christmas and February holidays. Their presence calmed me. I shared a bedroom with the youngest, who was called Diane. I liked looking after her. I felt a need to keep this little girl safe. The parents, sensing this, invited me to join them full-time between their various homes in Paris, Hong Kong and Honolulu, according to the season. My father vetoed the idea. The woman who had employed me called him, tried to reassure him, but he didn't want to hear about it – it was as if I were a deserter. There was something violent about his categorical refusal. How different my life would have been had I taken the job. In retaliation, I left school. I was determined to earn my own living, find my independence. I couldn't put up with my stepmother's attacks any more. Now that I was earning money she expected me to pay 350 francs for room and board every month. My father tried to object, but I knew he would never be able to protect us.

It wasn't until I was much older that I began to understand that she must have seen my mother in me, my father's great love with whom she could never compete, the beautiful face that surely haunted his long silences. He used to talk to me about Maman when we were alone, as if he were looking for something of my mother's presence in me.

I still carried her spirit within me. She was my strength as much as my sorrow. Nothing worse could ever happen to me, nothing could hurt me more than losing her, nothing could ever break me now. And I wanted to be happy. Not just brave, not just courageous, but happy, to make others happy too, to forge ahead, tirelessly, joyfully. Keeping watch over my mother, accomplishing all the simple things she had once dreamed of doing. Smiling, just as she is smiling in the few photos I still have of her.

FIVE

Pierre was waiting for us at the Gare de Lyon. Caroline sat in the front of the car, my grandson Maxime and I in the back. 'You'll finish your homework with Maminou,' said Pierre, glancing at the two of us in the rear-view mirror. It was his way of warding off bad luck, getting back to normal. What is left for a woman my age when she doesn't have a husband any more, just her children and grandchildren? But I couldn't only be Maminou, I just couldn't. I already was, of course, and I always will be, but I would never find peace simply by being an adjunct to my family's lives. I sensed it the moment we walked into their apartment. I didn't fit in. I hardly said a word.

Conversation at dinner that evening was dominated by everything that had happened. How could we avoid dwelling on it? The discussion revolved around the details furnished by the police, but there was so much more that loomed over us, the avalanche of what we were yet to see, the photographs and videos Deputy Sergeant Perret had told me about, and presumably David, Caroline and Florian as well. I had no intention of looking at any more of them. I knew enough. Dominique was nothing but a monster in the eyes of his children. It was heartbreaking to listen to them. I understood the shock, the pain, the terrible suspicions, I understood that the very foundations of our family were crumbling, but I did not want them to be destroyed. The children had been loved and cherished.

Deep down, I was like my dog, Lancôme. He was wandering around like a lost soul. He didn't understand what was happening. Caroline took an immediate dislike to him. She couldn't bear to have him in the apartment. 'He reminds me of *him*,' she said. Her father no longer had a name. 'I do not want that dog here!' she insisted. But I clung to him. He was the only thing I had left from the last few years. I walked him around the gardens, then brought him back up to the guest room where I was sleeping in my daughter's apartment.

I needed to be alone. To close the bedroom door. When I was on my own I breathed more easily, moved ahead at my own pace. I found my words, the thread of my history, an old story, deeply anchored in me, but now under attack from all sides by the police and my children. I could not erase everything in a single stroke. The last fifty years were so much more than a lie. Our first meeting in Aunt Andrée's kitchen, Dominique's shyness, our first night together in his parents' gloomy house, our crazy laughter even in adversity had not all been mere deception. Nor had his gentleness. When we were young, we used to talk for hours. He never tried to get the better of anyone. But as he grew older, he gained confidence. Then, it's true, he did start to get aggressive when he was contradicted – he didn't like being disagreed with – but that didn't worry me. I could hold my own against him and the children could too as they got older. He never raised a hand to them, and he had only been physically violent with me once, when he thought I was about to leave him. I was probably incapable of interpreting the evolution of his personality and his authoritarian outbursts, perhaps because they didn't stop him laughing with us, or singing in the car, or because they weren't in the form of commands. I would never have stayed with a tyrant. The last few months, on the other hand, had been difficult. He had begun raising his voice. 'You're just like your father,' I once said to him.

'And you are just like yours, like all the Guillous who bend over and take it.'

He actually said that to me one day, knowing full well how much it would hurt me. Could he feel the noose tightening? I needed to re-examine my life, to try and locate the moments, the signs that I had been unable to decipher. And why had my aches and pains, my memory lapses, my health concerns not been enough to make him stop?

Why had he joked that morning I'd called him in a desperate panic? I had told him it felt like when my waters had broken. I was having gynaecological problems on top of my memory lapses. And he quipped, 'What have you been getting up to during the day?' The leaking body of an ageing woman was suspect, and therefore the woman herself was suspect. I must have laughed with him, laughed with my torturer. Later he would tell the police and then the judge that he couldn't have hurt me because I was asleep. But whenever I called him, whenever I told him how exhausted I was, that I had a strange liquid leaking out of my vagina, there was something wrong; whenever I pinched the skin on the back of my hand to stop being engulfed by a blackout, to reassure myself that I could still feel – *Yes, you're still here, you're alive* – I was afraid, and he knew it. 'I'm doomed, Mino,' I used to tell him, convinced I was going to die like my mother. 'Don't be silly, it's nothing,' he reassured me. I spent a decade having endless medical examinations. Blood tests. Scans. Multiple courses of vaginal pessaries. Neurological tests. Ten years of going to see doctors who looked at me as if to say that at my age, a woman can't expect much any more, she ought to just relax and let time continue its demolition work. Never wondering what might be going on. Never attempting a diagnosis. And Dominique, always there by my side. He knew.

In fact, my health concerns had started around the time we moved to Mazan. Namely, after I stopped working and we began spending most of our time together. But how could I have suspected anything? When we first started contemplating retirement, we drew a circle on the map of France between Valence and Marseille. We decided that was where we wanted to go, to the sunshine in the South. We had both begun working so young that now we had years of leisure time to look forward to. He first suggested the Ariège department, but I said no, it was too far from everything. I wanted to be close to a city and to the high-speed train that would take me to Paris to see the children, and I wanted a swimming pool so they would come and stay in the holidays. I wanted to remain connected to them. Was he already plotting to isolate me? The splendour of the Vaucluse landscapes at the foot of Mont Ventoux settled the matter for us. We moved on

A HYMN TO LIFE

March 1st 2013. We were both sixty. Had he already planned it all out?

Yes, he had, as I later learned from the investigation. But that night in Caroline's apartment, and the ones that followed, I couldn't unravel it all. My mind was in disarray, filled with a cacophony that strangely took me back to our first years together. All those memories relentlessly flooding back, that feeling of being slammed on to the sand by the waves. I somehow had to protect those early days, to isolate the past from the present, to preserve that first spark, come what may. I couldn't have been so wrong about this man who was going to love me. I had believed it so strongly that I had heard it as a promise. I can still feel that sensation that swelled inside me the day I met him, it burns in me to this day, it hurts, but no one can take it away from me. He offered me the affection and confidence I lacked. He looked at me in a way that no one ever had, his eyes intense and his cheeks blushing. I was no longer the fat, ugly girl my stepmother endlessly denigrated. I was not going to drown in my father's grief-stricken eyes. All of a sudden I wasn't afraid of how other people saw me. Happiness had found me at last. Had found us.

Immediately after the wedding, Dominique and I moved in together near Paris. My father had found him a job as an electrician. I had found us a place to rent in Brunoy, in the Essonne. It was a one-bedroom apartment on the ground floor of a newly built three-storey building surrounded by gardens. I wanted to live somewhere rural for Dominique's sake; he had grown up among fields and trees. To begin with, we had nothing, just a mattress on the floor, with flattened cardboard boxes beneath it to insulate it from draughts coming through the floorboards. A camping stove to heat up our food. Dominique knocked together a wardrobe. Our impoverishment was the sign of our freedom. The price of our escape. We were always laughing. I wore the thigh-high white boots and miniskirts that were all the rage. I listened to the talk of the times, the fight for birth control, for legal abortion; I understood, but these were not my battles. My victory was building the kind of family life I had never had — that none of the people I loved had ever had.

A year later David was born. It was my suggestion to name him after the artist who had given the emperor's mother back to him. I stopped working. I didn't want anyone else to look after my son. Dominique was promoted to foreman with the industrial electrical company Trindel, and we received a government housing subsidy that helped us make it through to payday. We were happy. We had made it.

And yet. Whenever Dominique was called out for an emergency repair in the middle of the night, I always left the light on in our bedroom and switched on the radio to listen to a phone-in show on Europe 1 that came on at midnight called *Ligne Ouverte*, with Gonzague Saint Bris. I loved the opening music, Erik Satie's *Gnossienne No. 1*. Strangers called in to share their woes. I could have shared mine. I lay awake, waiting for Dominique to come home. I was afraid to fall asleep on my own.

That night at Caroline's it all came back to me. I can't remember in what order, I suppose the memories were flooding in all at once. Distant ones. Recent ones. How could he have ruined everything, thrown me to the wolves, sacrificed me? How could he have turned me into that inert, almost dead woman? I talked to him and to the children in turn, lying there alone in the dark. The children who used to say to us, 'Your childhood is straight out of a Zola novel!' They couldn't understand what had brought us together, how we had struggled, what we had achieved, what sinister undertow might have carried us off.

A battle was unleashed in my head. Between shadow and light. From the spark of our first meeting, I had ignited a flame. Must I blow it out now, once and for all, as David and Caroline seemed to be asking me to do? That would mean opening my eyes, finding myself desperately alone in the dark of the night, in a bedroom that was not my own, with nothing but my bulldog's ragged breathing for company. I couldn't face that. You don't get a second chance at life. If I erased everything, it would mean I was dead. And had been for years.

SIX

The next morning, there were so many things to do. First a blood test, to check for HIV, syphilis and herpes. All the nasties left by strangers' penises. I did it calmly, without panicking. My body did not remember anything; it was my body, but it was also not quite mine, the way you have no memory of the scalpel cutting into flesh when you come out of the operating theatre. I made an appointment with a psychologist in Versailles whose contact details my son-in-law Pierre had found. She understood the urgency. The appointment was scheduled for the following day.

In the meantime, Caroline called Florian to come and pick up the dog. He told her that if he was going to take Lancôme to his house he would take me too, because we couldn't be separated. Caroline was determined to take charge. She began going through the documents that we had hastily gathered together before leaving Mazan. The thick file containing the details of our debts shocked her. She turned the pages uneasily, looking through the loans, the eye-watering interest rates, the penalties. I tried to make light of it all. We had always had financial issues, it was just part of our life. She knew about them because her father sometimes called her to borrow small sums of money to avoid going over his overdraft limit, which he paid back later. But the harsh light of day changed everything, exposing our life ticking like a time bomb, and no doubt also bringing back painful memories, the buried fears that children repress in order not to add to their parents' woes. Caroline must have been eleven or twelve when she saw bailiffs and a removal truck turn up at our house and take everything away except the children's beds, their father powerless to stop them. He was unemployed at the time. I was at work. I remember my daughter's terrified expression when I came home. I tried to console her. 'It doesn't matter,' I said, 'it's only furniture, we can buy new things.' But she was deeply disturbed by the episode. I did what I always did, what people try to do when they have lost everything, stay strong, not fall apart, while she felt the ground swaying beneath her feet. No doubt this left her too vulnerable, caught between her father's powerlessness and her mother's apparent lack of concern.

It had all been waiting to resurface. We were replaying exactly the same scene, a few decades later, both of us adults now: she was panicking, and I was trying to keep things on an even keel. Dominique and I had always juggled with our finances. In 1999 we had even got divorced without actually separating, in order to avoid my salary being seized to cover Dominique's debts. We remarried in 2007. Maybe David, Caroline and Florian had assumed that everything had been cleared up, and their parents were a rare example of miraculous, inseparable coupledom.

The house in Mazan must have ended up convincing them. It was the perfect place for them and their children to spend their holidays. Opening up the French doors in the living room, watching the little ones run out into the garden to the swings or the hammocks rocking in the breeze, jump into the pool that we left uncovered all summer long, seeing them grow, learn to swim, gain confidence, and then, when night fell, tidying up all the delightful havoc they had wreaked – wet towels, pool noodles, inflatable slide, tangled garden hose – always gave me a wonderful feeling of serenity and accomplishment. Of course, it was all beyond our means, far too idyllic for our modest origins and Dominique's chaotic career. Obviously we didn't own the house. But nothing worried me as long as I could keep up with the 1,200-euro monthly rent. We lived on my pension while Dominique was paying back his debts. 'It seems like you're tightening your belts, you don't go anywhere any more,' David once said with concern. We replied that the splendours of Provence were enough for us.

Caroline was enraged. She kept screaming that her house and everything she owned were going to be seized because her father was insolvent and in prison. I tried to reason with her, she mustn't worry, no one was coming after her. I would set up a debt management plan in my own name. But my words only made things worse. Either I was irresponsible and blind, or I was guilty. Perhaps I was guilty – of promising them too much, a lovely life, the kind of security we'd never had. It was all a lie, as it turned out.

In the evening everything changed dramatically. Caroline discovered that someone had leaked some grim details about our story, although it was just a few vague lines in a local newspaper published in the South of France. She broke down. I had no words, I was completely exhausted, I no longer knew who I was, all I wanted to do was shut myself away with Maxime. Caroline rang Florian, who tried, in vain, to calm her. Pierre, her husband, was also unable to. I was so worried that I begged him to call an ambulance so she could be sedated. This time everyone thought it best to take her to hospital.

Caroline spent the night in the psychiatric unit. I slept at her apartment, in the guest room at the end of the corridor. She was terrified. I was too. Did she let out the screams that I held in, allowing herself to collapse as I did not?

I could have asked these questions, without hope of finding any answers. But that night, like the previous nights, I was simply hanging on, vainly seeking sleep. I refused to take a sleeping pill. Never again. All night long I delved back into my memories, talking to everyone in words I would be unable to articulate in the morning. Alone in my bed, I was outraged, I defended myself. I couldn't let my daughter claim we had behaved irresponsibly. I had always been so frugal. The white tennis shoes I kept until the soles wore through. The way I was so careful never to spend more than we could afford at the supermarket each week, even if it meant putting items back on the shelves. The way we never filled the car up with petrol, putting in just enough to get us through a few days at a time. We only filled the tank when the children came down to stay. We would go to the petrol station the day before they arrived and ask the pump attendant not to cash the cheque until the following month. We never wanted the children to feel limited or deprived of anything when they were with us. That was how we had always been, juggling overdrafts and loans to help pay for their studies, their weddings, their travels.

I lay awake, clinging to memories of gestures and objects, all the little things that fulfil us, or give us the illusion they do. It was so hard to see the whole picture now. I pleaded. And then, all at once, I was furious with myself. I was so angry that I hadn't noticed anything. One time in Mazan I had come close to the truth. On a pair of trousers I had just bought on sale, I noticed some odd, discoloured blotches like splashes of bleach, indelible, inexplicable. I tried to figure out what could have happened, to go over what I might have done or handled the day before. Nothing came to me. An immense fog shrouded the entire day. I couldn't remember a single thing. What time I got up, what I wore, what I ate, whether or not I left the house, absolutely nothing. I joked to Dominique, who was busy fixing something, 'Doumé, you haven't been drugging me, have you?'

He burst into tears. 'How could you possibly say such a thing?' I was instantly overcome with guilt. He was hurt. I immediately apologised. It was September 2013. This was not the first time I experienced a strange memory lapse, but it was the first time I really took note of it. I wonder now if perhaps, deep down, in some inaccessible part of me, I didn't entirely trust him, since I had accused him, albeit in the tone of a bad joke. So why did he begin to cry? To remind me of the pact against sorrow that had long ago sealed our commitment to each other? He was putting me off the scent. His tears should have alerted me. Now, unable to sleep, I began reviewing my life on an endless loop. It became a spiral, a tornado destroying everything in its path. But I clung to what I had loved. I would not succumb.

'You can't stay with your daughter,' said the psychologist the next day when I told her about Caroline's condition and her accusations. 'Do you have anywhere else you can go?'

'I could stay with my son.'

Florian came to fetch me. I took my two suitcases and my dog and moved in with him. I was exhausted. I was no longer in control of anything. I let things happen. The legal machine had been set in motion and was making decisions for me.

I now had a lawyer whom Caroline's husband, Pierre, had found a couple of days after the initial revelations. We spoke one evening on the telephone when I was still in Mazan, and met for the first time on my birthday, December 7th. I'm sure I wasn't what she was expecting. She had imagined either a woman in pieces, or a warrior. I was neither. I was a little disconcerted by her as well. She was blonde and wore an Hermès scarf around her neck like a good bourgeois Parisienne, but without the polish that usually goes with it. From the outset, she established a kind of camaraderie between us. For me, entering a world so unlike my own, this was both reassuring and disorienting. She called Caroline and me her '*petites chéries*', her little darlings. She talked about initiating divorce proceedings. I said yes, but just as when the police had asked me if I would be pressing charges, it hadn't actually occurred to me.

On December 14th, she and I met with the *juge d'instruction*, the examining magistrate, at the court in Avignon. We were early, so we went into a small side office to prepare for the meeting. Our lawyer pulled up some photographs from the case file. She wanted me to look at them, because the magistrate would undoubtedly confront me with them. Up until then I had only seen the three they had shown me at the police station. She scrolled through several more. Always the bedroom. Always me, lifeless, a man raping me. Only the dates and the names of the criminals changed. I stopped her. I didn't want to see any more. She took out the two photographs of Caroline. I had not seen them before. They'd been taken in the dark. My heart clenched. I didn't recognise her straight away. She is lying on her side, her face in shadow. In one picture she wears a sweatshirt, in the other a tank top and a pair of beige underpants. Her body does not look completely limp; her arms are drawn together as if she's asleep in the foetal position, whereas in the photographs of me, mine flop open like a broken marionette. The photographs are abject, showing her father's unbearable incestuous gaze on his daughter while she slept. I peered more closely, trying to recognise the room where they had been taken and to work out what year it could have been. No matter how hard I tried, I could not think of a time they had ever been alone under the same roof. Where were we? Where was I? The darkness of the images made it impossible to answer immediately.

Basically, we were both looking at them from the perspective of who we were: I was warding off the worst-case scenario, while my daughter was heading straight for it. '*Mes petites chéries*,' she called us. Her little darlings.

Eventually we were summoned to the office of the examining magistrate, Gwenola Journot. She was so young that at first I thought she was the court clerk. But then the clerk came in and she was even younger. I was old enough to be their mother. Imagining them looking at the photos and videos that I refused to see made me feel ashamed, and now in their presence I felt the modesty of an older woman. I had never been afraid of growing old, but here I was, trapped in the image others had of me. I wanted the two young women not to see the pictures; I wanted to protect them from these horrors, as I was protecting myself.

The magistrate asked if I had anything to add to what I had already told the police. I told her about the jigsaw puzzle in my head that I was relentlessly trying to piece together and then take apart, day and night, the thousands of elements I was trying to make sense of, in vain. Of course, I didn't tell her about the good memories, which she had no interest in and which even my children didn't want to hear about. I kept these to myself, to wrap myself in like a blanket to ward off the cold. I told her about all the incidents that I now realised were signals I had missed. My odd little joke when I discovered bleach stains on my yellow trousers. The cocktail he handed me that he hurriedly emptied into the sink when I said it tasted peculiar. The glass of beer that had turned green. I had to pinpoint each event to be able to date it and work out when it had all started. The incident with the cocktail was when we were living in Villiers-sur-Marne. Which meant that the poisoning had begun at least as long ago as 2011.

The magistrate knew far more than I did anyway. The photographs and videos in her file had been classified, numbered and dated. All I had was the hazy memory of my blackouts, my concerned children and friends saying, 'Don't you remember our conversation?' That is how I discovered that he had drugged me on October 3rd 2020 – after he was arrested for upskirting in the supermarket, after his confession, his weeping, his promises to me, his tears at the thought of losing me. And then again, on the 10th and then the 21st, the night I got back from Paris after I'd been looking after David's children. I remember that day very clearly. Dominique came to pick me up at the station. We got back to the house at 4 p.m. and I was surprised to find dinner already in the oven. He had made mashed potatoes in two separate dishes, since he liked his with butter and I liked mine with olive oil and parsley. He had added lorazepam and zolpidem to mine. We ate early. I have no memory whatsoever of what happened after that. I realised in the magistrate's office that the rapes had become more frequent in October. He must have known they would be his last; the police had seized his phone and computer, and he knew they would have found his photographs and videos. He knew that the moment he entered the police station on November 2nd he would not leave it as a free man. And I would never again be the plaything of his barbaric fantasies.

'What was your sex life with Monsieur Pelicot like?' the magistrate asked me. It had become a question I found difficult to answer. I had always thought we had a normal sex life, perhaps better than most couples our age. We still made love five or six times a month. It was mostly on his initiative. His sexual appetite had always been bigger than mine, but that fitted with the notion I had of men and women.

He had changed a great deal over fifty years. The initial signs, I realise now, came with my pregnancies. A first pregnancy is an exhilarating and daunting adventure, and he was always by my side, considerate, overjoyed at the birth of David, who was born in a matter of minutes. He was just as happy during the second. He really wanted children. But one day he told me pregnant women aren't pretty. I must have said something in reply, but what I remember is feeling the sting, or rather the chill, of a male gaze concerned only with his own desire. For my body was swelling, becoming more bestial. On the day of Caroline's birth, my labour went on so long that Dominique had to go back to work. Epidurals were uncommon at the time, and I didn't have one with either birth. I was left alone to endure the contractions that were ripping my pelvis apart. I was exhausted, mumbling about how afraid I was of dying, and then she arrived, a wonderful little baby girl, and all my fears evaporated.

I loved breastfeeding my babies, bonding with them and being needed. I loved their smell, their softness. I loved covering them with kisses. I loved being a mother. I was emotional, overwhelmed, worn out, my body still aching from the delivery. I had no energy for anything apart from my daughter and her big brother.

After the children were born Dominique became more insistent, as though seeing me monopolised by motherhood made him want to pull me back to him. He was impatient for our sex life to resume. The mother had taken his wife away from him.

As my strength and desire slowly returned, Dominique suggested something new: fellatio. I was twenty-seven and had no idea what that was. I had grown up in a body I did not like, being constantly attacked by my stepmother for my appearance, and obviously I was never taught anything about sex. Like so many young women of my generation, I had rushed into marriage with the idea that love and family would save me, though I didn't think of it in those terms at the time. They were beliefs inculcated in us so young that they governed the way we lived, insinuated themselves into our minds. Perhaps they ran even deeper in me; I was not looking for a conventional life, but for profound consolation. I married my first lover when he was an awkward and shy young man. Now he wanted fellatio. I started doing it. Was it to please him? Yes. But it didn't feel like I was submitting to a demand. It felt like part of our evolving relationship, a way of keeping it alive and giving him pleasure, the same way we loved to laugh, dance, travel and live together. Then he began asking for more. 'There's a part of you I don't possess,' he said. He meant anal sex.

'Never,' I said. He didn't insist. So I was able to refuse. He did not always get what he wanted.

I also told him to throw away his sex toys, but he obviously didn't, because the magistrate informed me that they'd been found by the police. Though I was taken aback by her youth I was reassured by the fact that she was a woman. Maybe, like everyone else, she thought I didn't seem distressed enough, vindictive enough, angry enough. Maybe she found me naive. I told her that despite our various problems, I had always thought we were happy. 'I was content with my simple little life.' That's how I put it. In my little life, there were highs and lows, and men who thought about sex more than women. It was a natural law as old as time. When my daughter-in-law Aurore, Florian's partner, walked in on Dominique masturbating in his office, she confided her embarrassment to Florian, who in turn spoke to me about it. I immediately broached the subject with Dominique, and he replied, 'All guys do it.' I didn't know what to say. I'm sure I would have been horrified at what he was looking at, but we didn't know anything about that then and I only used the computer to do my accounts. I had no interest in the internet and social media, and I had no idea of the extent to which they had altered human relationships. In my little life, I always thought that a dangerous man was by definition aggressive, which Dominique wasn't.

It's true that over the previous few months, maybe even the previous few years, our sex life had become less tender. He always preferred to penetrate me from behind, not to meet my eyes. What was that about? Regret? Shame? What was he thinking of when he looked at me? Us? His fantasies? He once suggested I have a Brazilian wax, which I also refused.

'What are your feelings today about Dominique Pelicot?' asked the examining magistrate.

'He disgusts me, I feel dirty, soiled, betrayed.'

These are the words that appear in the interview transcript. My faltering and hesitations have been cut. Justice needs to keep moving along. Sometimes I call him 'my husband' and immediately correct myself, and say 'he' as Caroline does. Or 'Monsieur', as though speaking of a stranger. In one instance, it is noted that I am crying. That is the moment I tell the magistrate I have lost everything. It is the desolation, the collapse, the arrival at the Gare de Lyon that bring me to tears, not what all those men did to me. I don't remember anything about that. The magistrate asked me if I wanted to see some of the videos. I categorically refused. Over the past few weeks, I had been spending an absurd amount of time in the shower, obsessively washing myself, scrubbing myself clean of the filth of all those men who had raped a dead woman. That was the impression I had got from the few photographs I had seen: sleep and death conflated.

A few days later, I had an appointment at the forensic medicine unit in Versailles. My body was a piece of evidence. Anne Martinat Sainte-Beuve, the medical examiner, told me that analysis of my hair had revealed traces of drugs despite the fact that I had been dyeing it regularly for years. This was evidence of extremely high levels of intoxication. She asked me a series of questions about the regularity and intensity of my blackouts. I answered calmly. I was feeling much better. I was no longer having blackouts, which meant that my condition was reversible, and proof that if I stayed away from him, I would be fine.

I already knew that, but had no idea how to interpret it all. Dominique had always made sure to do that for me. He often said that I had given so much to the children that my exhausted body couldn't help decompressing when I got home. His brother, Joël – a doctor, no less – agreed. 'The brain knows best. It's like how the vacuum cleaner switches off when the bag is full,' he said when I told him about my blackouts. Let's not dwell on the comparison between a woman's brain and a vacuum cleaner bag. I'd known Dominique's family long enough not to be offended. Joël's vulgarity only emphasised his brother's tenderness, which was how I had always thought of him, and was what made him so different from all the other Pelicot men. I still believed this was true of Dominique when he started accompanying me to the doctor. He was the one who made the appointments. He wanted to reassure me. I hadn't realised the way he controlled my emotions, the way he'd give the answer to a question that I had not even thought of asking. The way he somehow ensured that I brought up my health concerns as rarely as possible with my daughter and sons. 'You don't want to worry them,' he would say. How did I persist in seeing kindness where there was nothing but manipulation?

It was not until around 9 p.m. that I at last entered the gynaecological examination room. It was late for us both, the doctor and me. She was having trouble attaching the stirrups to the examination table. When she finally succeeded, I slipped my feet into them, as all women have done at least once in their lives. Our bare feet on cold metal, our bare buttocks on the edge of the table, our legs spread to reveal that part of our bodies that we ourselves never see. I have done so many of these examinations over the last few years, at an age when in theory a woman has fewer reasons to see a gynaecologist. No more need for contraception, no more children to look forward to. Just a waning libido, the aches and pains of a body that is drying up, and the need to keep an eye out for cancer.

The first speculum hurt. She went to look for a smaller one. She couldn't see any tearing. On top of the sleeping pills, Dominique always gave me a powerful muscle relaxant so my body slackened and dilated, which is why I never felt any pain the following day. This was something she asked me about, as so many other women later would similarly wonder when they heard my story. At this point, my children and I were the only ones grappling with that question.

The many doctors I had consulted up until then had never taken the kind of swabs she did. Nor had they ever thought to check for STDs. I had been treated for an inflamed cervix and instructed to stop having sex once and for all. These new tests revealed the presence of countless bacteria and of a papillomavirus that would need to be monitored, because it could develop into cancer. I was prescribed powerful antibiotics. As far as everything else was concerned, I did not have Alzheimer's and I did not have a brain tumour like my mother. Life was sending me contradictory messages: my entire life had fallen apart, but I was fine.

*

I gave notice to my landlady for the middle of February. The next thing was to empty the house. Florian was going to take the leather couch, the bicycle and the scooter. It made sense to give him these things because he was also in the throes of moving. He rented a van and the two of us drove down to Mazan at the end of December. Inside the house, everything was just as we had left it a month earlier. I had to dig deep to summon the strength to walk through the rooms.

After my mother's death, all the furniture in our house had been draped in white sheets. In Mazan, whatever we didn't keep would be sold off cheaply on the website Leboncoin. We took photos. We quoted very low prices so that everything would go quickly. Sylvie agreed to be there to open the front door to potential buyers. Double-door fridge: 80 euros. Induction hob: 40 euros. Bed: 80 euros – yes, the brand-new bed that belonged to Monsieur and Madame Pelicot, the bed of horrors. Is that where I had died?

I put together a pile of things for Dominique. He hadn't received anything since the small bag I had hastily packed at the request of the police for his time in custody. He was now incarcerated in the prison in Le Pontet, near Avignon. Winter was coming. I was worried about him being cold. I wanted to see him, to ask him all the questions that troubled me during the day and kept me awake at night, to talk about the sense of ruin and waste that haunted me. He was probably the only person who would understand. But for legal reasons I was not allowed to see him. I gathered items that he would need: a towel, pyjamas, a pair of shoes, socks, underwear, a jumper to keep him warm. I couldn't find his contact lenses. I put everything in a rubbish bag, because I knew he was not allowed a suitcase. Florian came with me to Le Pontet to drop it off. When we arrived, the prison officer at the front desk told us that the bag was not regulation, and pointed us in the direction of a nearby shop where I could buy a soft shopping bag. It was emblazoned with patches from different countries around the world and closed with a large zip.

   I packed everything neatly inside and we headed back to the prison. We deposited the bag at the reception desk and left. We stood for a long time in front of the grey building, looking up at it and wondering if he was behind one of the windows, if he was watching us. We still felt very connected to him. At least I did.

SEVEN

When Dominique and I first began living together, it felt as if we had escaped our misfortune, left it all behind along with the chateaux and forests of the Indre, and the tears of Juliette, Dominique's mother, who wept uncontrollably whenever we went to visit her. She dwelled incessantly on the past, on her long road as a Pelicot, the name I had just taken. I never saw her as anything other than a victim, a wife cowering in the background, terrified of her husband. I couldn't discern the slightest trace of emotion or repressed dreams in this little woman who was barely five feet tall. She dyed her hair, but it didn't soften the fatigue and resignation that marked her face. I felt centuries apart from her.

Juliette was married to André, the eldest of the Pelicot brothers, until one day, out of the blue, he walked out on her, leaving her alone with no financial resources and two young children to care for. Denis, André's youngest brother, set his sights on his forsaken sister-in-law. He was only seventeen. She was ten years his senior. She fell pregnant so quickly that the divorce had not yet been finalised, so Joël, their first son, was registered as André's son. It was the law that a wife could only fall pregnant by her husband. It was like a bad omen presaging the chain of abuse from one brother to the next.

Dominique was born four years later and formally recognised as the son of Denis and Juliette Pelicot.

When I became part of the family, Juliette was still cleaning houses, having been a factory worker for Kodak before becoming an Avon Lady, selling cosmetics door-to-door. Denis Pelicot drove around in an Arthur Martin appliance repair truck and didn't work very much. Some days he would park the truck and sit inside it all day reading a book from the library. He was always home early. His imposing stature, moustache and loud voice brought a chill into the house. He was all-powerful there. In the outside world he went from job to job, never committing or finding stability, and no one ever knew whether he had left or been fired.

During the early years of their marriage, Denis Pelicot ran a small hotel and restaurant called La Croix Blanche in Mamers, a little town in the Sarthe. But the place was on its last legs, and after a few years he dragged his wife and children to the Indre, where they moved into a house in the grounds of the Château d'Oublaise. Another chateau, this one a huge, turreted castle that after World War Two had been turned into a retirement home for veterans of the armoured cavalry division. A lair for disabled ex-servicemen, deep in the forest. Later, severely wounded soldiers and ex-legionnaires from the colonial wars were housed there alongside WWII veterans. With time, peace and prosperity, the notion of disability was broadened, and veterans who had been in prison, or had mental health problems, or didn't have two sous to rub together, or drank too much, were also given room and board.

A HYMN TO LIFE

The Château d'Oublaise became a shelter for anyone who did not fit into a rapidly changing society. There were many such men, and the establishment grew so large that it was talked about on the radio. Dominique's father first learned about the place when he heard the writer and radio presenter Pierre Bellemare discussing it. Apparently there was work to be had there. He must have sensed that there were vulnerable people and a domain over which he could rule. He applied and was taken on as warden.

The family moved into a small house in the grounds. Dominique was seven. He spent a lot of time on his own. His older siblings, Geneviève and André, had already left home. Quite soon Joël started boarding at the Lycée Giraudoux in Châteauroux and only came home at weekends. Dominique was trapped with his mother and father, living amid the comings and goings of physically fragile or mentally disturbed men. He cycled a long way through the countryside to school in the nearest village. His classmates called him the kid from Oublaise. He became an outcast, ostracised for the theft of a sweet that had actually been stolen by the pharmacist's son. After school he would go back to the chateau and play football for hours with his imaginary teammates. That was his escape. Football became his lifelong passion. We had a photograph at Mazan of him aged nine in a black jersey, shorts and studded boots. It must have been destroyed in the frenzy of my children's rage. There in the woods, surrounded by all those lost souls, some part of him was shaped. He still had memories and childlike impressions that he used to tell me about. Like the evening he got lost in the forest on his way to fetch milk, or his fear on the stormy night when his parents were away and he sought refuge in the room of one of the residents of the chateau, even though he had been warned never to go anywhere near him. The man gave him some chocolate, and when his parents got back, Denis gave him hell. Denis Pelicot doled out discipline according to rules and whims that were his alone. He used corporal punishment. Of all the dangers that threatened Dominique, the most fearsome was his father.

'Leave him,' Dominique told his mother.

The first time he said it he was fourteen and had just started his first job. After that he told her to leave his father many times, but she never did. She probably never even considered it. She was ten years older than her husband, and he was starting to make her pay for it. Juliette was mired in unhappiness.

'She loved him, she was really in love with Denis, she'd have accepted anything,' Dominique's half-sister, Geneviève, told me recently over the phone. What options did she have? Geneviève knows what it was like to grow up in Denis Pelicot's terrifying house. She never went into detail about what went on there, but she said at the trial something she had often said to me in the past, 'He'd have liked to have the daughter.' She was talking about herself. She had fled, got married very young just to escape his grasp. How could any of us help wondering if things might have turned out differently had Juliette left Denis, had she managed to pick herself up and escape too?

Denis Pelicot made yet another fresh start. He was hired

as a repair man by Debiard, a household appliances firm. The family moved to 90, route de Tours, an apartment in a three-storey council-owned building in Châtillon-sur-Indre. To make ends meet, they took in Nicole, a little girl with learning disabilities who was a ward of the state. She was five. She probably didn't expect much from her new foster family, given that she had been beaten in her previous foster homes. She clung to a doll that she would not let go of for anything in the world, an imaginary friend who was supposed to protect her.

These were the people I was to get to know several years later. A month after we first met at my aunt's house in July 1971, I joined Dominique on a camping trip to the Ile d'Oléron with his parents, his half-brother and wife, and Nicole, still clutching her doll. We were nineteen, thus still legally underage. We were not allowed to sleep in the same tent, but every evening we liked to spread out a blanket on the sand and watch the lights on the coast. I joined them again the following summer. I even brought along my brother, Michel. Denis was incensed when I laid my mattress next to Dominique's in the tent. 'They're sleeping together!' he bellowed. He tried to stop us. We didn't give in. But it was Juliette who paid the price. He refused to address a single word to her, except to issue demands.

It was during another such camping holiday one summer several years earlier that a younger Dominique had apparently surprised his parents in their tent: his mother on her knees, hands tied behind her back, being forced to fellate her husband. He never told me about it. I only found out during the trial.

Whenever I spent time with the Pelicots, I understood a little more about where the man I loved came from, what he was fleeing, why he always used to stay so late at Aunt Andrée's house.

When Dominique decided to join me in Paris, he communicated his decision to his father on a slip of paper that he placed inside his shaving kit. He didn't dare tell him in person. Leaving, for him, was synonymous with escape. It also meant less income for his family, because he had been paying his salary in full over to his parents. He did have his own bank account with Crédit Agricole, into which I had been putting a little aside every month for our future together. But because he was only nineteen, his father still controlled his account, and when he got wind of our plans he emptied it. He bought a small farm called La Thibaudière and insisted Dominique do the renovations. I still have this image in my mind of Dominique right at the bottom of the well, as though he would never be able to climb out again and was going to let himself be buried alive by his father, who was still trying to control our future. He stole from us, and we said nothing. Just as I said nothing when Papa came to meet him, and Denis Pelicot announced that he and his wife could not afford a sit-down lunch for our wedding. Papa tried to insist, he wanted a fitting celebration for his daughter, nothing fancy, just my uncles, my aunts, his family and Maman's family sitting together at long tables draped with white tablecloths. Dominique's mother said she would roast some chickens and that was it. She did what she was told. I did too. I said it didn't matter, it would be fine like that. It wasn't true. We had a dreary picnic lunch, but I couldn't face yet another fight, I just wanted to get married so we could live together. Escape at last. I let Denis Pelicot trample on my father's only request. He frightened me too.

I have never forgotten the way he looked at me when we came to visit the following year. I was in my bathing costume outside in the yard of the new farm, pregnant with David, combing my hair, which at the time went down past my waist. As I turned I saw him through the window sitting on his bed, watching me. Something in his expression made me feel deeply ill at ease. I mentioned it later to Dominique. He wasn't surprised, he was the ogre's son, after all. The following summer, his brother groped my backside. The older boy was just like his father, but Dominique was different. He was nothing like either of them. He was close to his mother in her silent suffering. A loving young father who got up in the night to give his son a bottle. And we were happy. We took David everywhere with us, even out to friends' houses in the evening. He was such an easy child. I remember how, aged three, he used to fall asleep, curled up on the floor underneath the table where we were playing board games. We had left, moved far away from the Indre and his family's brutality. We had joined the ranks of the growing middle classes in the suburbs of Paris. And for years, every Sunday morning, Dominique would take the children out to the forest in Sénart and play endless games of football with them, as if, at last, he'd found the playmates he'd never had when he lived at Oublaise.

As time passed, I stopped believing we mirrored each other. I was protecting him. I knew that where he came from, nobody offered comfort to anyone else. Only tyranny held his family together. I began to understand how different we were. In his case, there was a constant threat of violence and, significantly, it came from within the family. For me, the tragedy belonged to the past; it left us inconsolable, but full of lost love.

My brother had grown into a taciturn, resigned young man. He worked as a plumber on construction sites and let slip no other details about his life. My father, under pressure from my stepmother, had moved to Brittany, where he was born. I was sad that he would no longer live nearby, now that David had just been born. I wanted him to be close to me and my children. 'Papa, you're leaving?' His resigned expression was his only answer. His wife called him Younic – Yves in Breton – or simply Youn. Like many other former soldiers, he worked recruiting labourers for the construction industry. One day his secretary found him collapsed on the floor of his office in Quimper. An aneurism that might burst at any moment had triggered an epileptic fit. He had emergency surgery but when he awoke from the operation he was paralysed on his left side. He was forty-seven. He learned to walk again, but his left arm remained lifeless. He would pick it up with his good hand and place it on his leg when he was sitting down, or slip it into his pocket. Half of him was no longer there, perhaps even more. But he was still elegant; he wore his suits well and never forgot cufflinks. And of course he still talked to me about my mother when we were alone. He would reminisce about her gentleness and her *joie de vivre*. She was his greatest loss, and my guiding light. By moving away, my father added to the absences in my life; he seemed to say that he didn't have much to offer any more, and that a new arrival offered no consolation for loss.

Caroline was born in January 1979. A baby girl. I don't know why but I was surprised. A few people wanted me to call her Jeanne, after my mother, but it was out of the question for me to bequeath her the legacy of a life so cruelly cut short. I came up with the name Caroline because of Princess Caroline of Monaco, I thought it sounded nice with Pelicot. We were ennobling the family name, writing a whole new history. And I can still see Caroline, looking adorable with her princess tiara in her hair, twirling her dress at the school fete. That day her grandmother Juliette was with us; she adored her granddaughter. And David had formed a close bond with his grandfather, who introduced him to his beloved westerns.

Despite our difficult memories, Dominique's parents occasionally came and stayed with us for a few days, and the children would sometimes go to them during the school holidays. They would meet up with their cousins and explore the landscapes that Michel and I had explored at the same age. We had left, but hadn't really managed to get away. We were born after the war, and throughout our childhood we had always sensed its shadow over the adults around us. Something made them tighten their jaws and quickly lose patience. They never talked about it, and we in turn never talked about how it affected us. They instilled in us a kind of fatalism. The most important thing for us was to live differently to our parents. We probably thought we could fix everything with our happiness and our wonderful children. Then one day, when David was eight, he told me that his grandfather had shut Caroline up in the dark with the goats because she wouldn't eat her dinner. My blood ran cold. I rang and told them they would never see their grandchildren again. We stopped going to La Thibaudière. But Juliette missed them terribly. She was sad, and of course Dominique was sensitive to that. So eventually we returned.

Nicole was now an adult. I said to my father-in-law I was surprised that she never went out or saw more people. I had gained a little confidence over the years. 'It's none of your business. Don't you go putting ideas in her head,' he snarled. We began to wonder. Was he abusing her? What better victim than a mentally disabled young woman without any family? Was he abusing her in front of his wife? Dominique tried to talk about it to his brother, Joël, who apparently brushed it aside and told him that incest happens in all families, rich and poor. He would know, of course, being a doctor. It seemed that for him incest was unremarkable, but for me it was the first time I had even heard the word. Joël was embarking on a political career with the local branch of the right-wing party Rally for the Republic; it was out of the question to risk a scandal in the family that might taint his pedigree. We said and did nothing, like everyone else who lived under Denis Pelicot's roof. We heard Juliette weeping. She asked us to lend her a bit of money. Dominique slipped her a few banknotes and I paid their electricity bill. It was almost as if our happiness, in order to exist, had to pay a tithe to misfortune.

When she was diagnosed with breast cancer, Juliette Pelicot realised that this would be her escape at last. In early 1986 I called to tell her I was pregnant again.

'I'm due in October, Juliette. Hang in there.'

'I won't be around by then,' she said. She died in the hospital, alone, with no one at her bedside, a few days before her sixty-fifth birthday. As was the custom back then, her body was brought back to the house for the wake. In the coffin, wearing a cancer wig, she finally looked at peace.

As soon as she was buried Denis Pelicot made his relationship with Nicole official. Nicole was twenty-five, he was fifty-eight. 'It does you no end of good to have a young thing in your bed,' he said.

Florian was born that October.

Something about Dominique was changing. It was as if up until then he had dissolved his pain into his mother's. Now she was gone, something burst. Memories began flooding back. He told me about a long-ago quarrel back in Oublaise with Joël, who had thrown a rock at him and hit him on the head. Dominique was eight. He was taken to the hospital in Châteauroux and kept overnight for observation. In the middle of the night he woke up, unable to breathe. When he opened his eyes, he thought he saw a moustache – that was how he said it, like a child. The penis of a male nurse was in his mouth. We had been married almost fifteen years and he had never told me this before. We began paying visits to La Thibaudière less and less often.

Denis Pelicot died of a heart attack in February 2004. Nicole found him on the kitchen floor. Dominique went to view the body, but did not attend the funeral. We had a trip planned to the Antilles. The children went. They knew, deep down, this man's significance for his son, the shadow he cast on him, and on them.

Several years later, Caroline asked her father to write about his childhood. She sensed that there were knots to be untangled, which writing might help him process. Dominique followed her advice. He gave me what he had written to read, and he also gave a copy to David, Caroline and Florian, and Geneviève. I don't have our copy any more. It was destroyed by the children that night in Mazan. Caroline's was deposited in the police case file. The text is suffused with his mother's suffering and his father's violence. He writes about the Château d'Oublaise, a rock thrown at his head, Nicole, and many other things. It ends with our first encounter. For him, he writes, meeting me signalled the end of the nightmare.

EIGHT

In the beginning we had love, freedom and the song by Michel Fugain that we sang at the tops of our voices as if it had been written especially for us: 'Une belle histoire'. Yes, ours had been a beautiful story and it haunted me now. It was both painful and vital. I needed what had been. I needed people who could listen, who believed it, who might even share it with me. My children couldn't. They had dumped the past at a recycling centre where everything is separated into glass, paper and plastic, but they were unable to distinguish their father from the poisoner and the rapist.

'You've had such a shitty life,' Caroline said.

No, that wasn't true.

Her intuition was good though. It was she who told Deputy Sergeant Perret about Pascale, when he was trying to find witnesses to my relationship with Dominique. Caroline remembered this friend of her parents who had mysteriously vanished from their lives. She even recalled how strange and abrupt it had been. Perret asked me to try and find Pascale. What a good idea. All of a sudden it felt terribly urgent to speak to her. We'd met in 1982 when we were both working for EDF. It had almost been like falling in love – one of those friendships that came out of nowhere and within a matter of days I couldn't imagine not having her in my life.

She was twenty and I was thirty, married with two children. She nicknamed me Pelic. Usually it's the men who call each other by their surnames. The way she did it, the way she amputated the last syllable, gave it a different consonance, lighter somehow. We began going out in the evenings. I'd leave Dominique at home with the children. She loved being invited over too. It was like having a younger sister. She was friends with my husband and the children were always excited when she came over to our house. She went on holiday with us.

And then, around the turn of the new millennium, I ended the friendship. She walked into my office one day when I had just got off the phone with Dominique. I must have said something nice about him, because she cut me short. 'Ah, your Doumé, you put him on a pedestal, but you have no idea what kind of a person you're living with.'

I was livid. I didn't even try to figure out what she meant. 'Get out of my office. I never want to see you again,' I hissed. I preferred to lose a dear friend than to understand. For the next eleven years, Pascale and I would pass each other in the corridor without even saying hello. I spoke to her briefly after I heard about the death of her mother, of whom I had been very fond. She sent me a card when I retired. Neither of us responded to the other one. And our paths never crossed again. It had been twenty years since we'd last spoken.

I contacted some former colleagues to see if anyone could put us in touch. I was doing it more for myself than for the police. With Pascale, I could go back in time. She wouldn't trample on my old memories. I wanted to hear what she had to say. I wanted her to explain what she had meant that day in my office, for the most painful aspect of what I was going through now was that I had not noticed anything back then. Every so often I found myself fantasising that I might have prevented it all, I might have saved us.

Eventually I got hold of her number. One morning at Florian's, after breakfast, I called her.

'Pascale, do you remember me? It's Gisèle Pelicot.'

'Pelic! How could I forget you?'

She sounded so happy to hear from me. Afterwards she told me that when she first heard my voice she thought Dominique must have died. She was convinced I would never have called her while he was still alive. In a way she was right. The man she had known, the man I had loved, no longer existed.

I said I needed to know what had happened. She told me he was always hitting on her. He sent her flowers after he'd done some work on her kitchen. One time when we were all on holiday together in Spain, he had held her in his arms after she had fainted and then told her he hoped to do it again. That was what she had been trying to tell me. Nothing that foretold the rapist of Mazan, just the pathetic, banal tale of a cheating husband playing footsie with his wife's younger friend.

I told her what was going on. She listened to me in absolute stupefaction, without painting me as submissive or a slave. She knew my life and our relationship. She remembered being all of twenty years old, telling me she hoped to meet a wonderful man too, to find her own Dominique. She was able to understand where I was – the icy, suffocating fog I was moving through. We talked for a long time. She told me how her life had turned out, about the various jobs and boyfriends she'd had. She said she had never been in a relationship as strong as mine and Dominique's. It was as if, despite the horrors I had just found out, the impressions and words from an earlier time could not be erased, were being expressed one last time. I could breathe again. I no longer felt so alone.

Three days later, she called back. She suggested that I pack a bag and come and stay the following weekend. We had found each other again.

The first night at her house we stayed up talking until five in the morning. Being with her opened the door to good memories, all those fulfilling, exhausting years when we were building our lives. When we had first met at EDF, Pascale was a very young administrative assistant and I was temping for three months as a secretary in the executive division. Our friendship could well not have lasted. I wasn't intending to stay. I even turned my nose up at the offer of a permanent position. I liked temping, moving from one company to the next, never committing, having time with the children. All I cared about was my family. I had given up work when David and Caroline were small to look after them. I was cautious, I thought we would just squeeze up a bit more in our little two-room apartment. I had nightmares sometimes. I would see tanks bearing down on Brunoy, the same tanks I had seen as a child in the streets of Reutlingen. I don't know what it meant, except perhaps that now I was a young mother, like Maman back in Germany just after the war, I was aware that everything was fragile, that I could die, lose everything.

But EDF kept pushing me to stay. Dominique too. We needed to get ahead. He was looking for a change as well, he didn't want to carry on being an electrician; he wanted to get away from the building sites his father had long made him work on to bring home a wage every week. He was hungry for something different, something bigger, and he had set his sights on us buying a house, becoming homeowners by the time we were thirty. A regular income would help. In October 1982 I finally signed a permanent contract with EDF. I started on the lowest rung of the secretarial ladder but was soon sent for training on a new kind of typewriter with a memory capacity — in other words, one of the first word processors. The only qualification I had was the school certificate I'd been awarded when I was fourteen, and all I had ever wanted was to have a family. Yet here I was getting to grips with the cutting-edge technology of the time.

I liked office life. I found it easy to get along with people. I grew in confidence. When I began working for EDF the headquarters were on rue de Miromesnil, near the Parc Monceau in Paris, before they moved to nearby rue d'Aguesseau. Every morning I squeezed on to a packed commuter train bound for Paris. We had moved out of our little apartment in Brunoy and bought a house in Combs-la-Ville. I had hesitated, I wasn't sure we could afford it. Dominique was moving too fast: we had to get a new car, we had to own our own home. I didn't care about any of that, I didn't need material comforts. When I reflect back on that period now, I think that I must have retained something of the beginnings of our relationship, our fragility, or perhaps the fragility I detected in him that so touched me. I wanted to slow down. After endless discussion, I gave in. But then I was convinced we had made a terrible mistake. I burst into tears, ruining our outing to Flunch in the Evry shopping centre where the children loved sliding their trays along the metal rails of the self-service queue as they greedily chose from the profusion of main dishes and desserts on offer. I had been trying to contain my anxiety, a strange feeling, difficult to define, the impression that I wasn't in control, that I couldn't leave the decision up to Dominique, that I couldn't put our lives in his hands. I burst into heaving sobs that I couldn't explain to him or the children; I just said that I was afraid that it was too much for us, that this stone house was too beautiful for us and we were never going to be able to pay off the mortgage. As if wanting more in life was theft. It was too much of a risk. But the bank had given us the green light and agreed to the loan. We would be living on credit, as the modern world invited us to do, with its new housing estates and shopping centres popping up on the outskirts of big cities for people like us. It seemed to be saying that all we had to do was go with the flow, fill our shopping trolleys at Euromarché and treat the family to a meal at Flunch with all-you-can-eat chips and endless whipped cream from the self-service machine. It promised us abundance. And with all this, we would allay our old childhood fears.

My time was divided. I was pulled in all directions. Work, family, constantly running around. I kept an eye on the children's education. David was beginning to lose interest in school, and I dreaded Friday evenings when his homework notebook was always empty. I'd ring the doorbell of one of his friends, copy down his homework for the weekend, and then make sure he did it. Sometimes I lost my temper because I was so worried about him, and then I'd be consumed with guilt for not staying calm.

Dominique had stopped working as an electrician. He had finally taken the plunge and moved into property, cutting his teeth in an estate agency in the 13th arrondissement in Paris. It was a start. He wore a suit and tie to work. He had to make deals, bring in business. His income was irregular and unpredictable, he only received an advance on potential future commissions. It took him three months to land his first sale.

He became more demanding sexually. He wanted new experiences, started suggesting things he had seen in porn magazines. I resisted, I wasn't like that. 'You're such a saint, you could have gone into a convent, you've got no fantasy life,' he said. It annoyed me but I wasn't worried. I recognised the condescending attitudes and smiles of those who revelled in excess – the heavy drinkers and sex enthusiasts deemed to be *bon vivants*. Mostly I thought of this as the natural inclinations of a man.

He was no longer my blushing teenage sweetheart. He was athletic, very physical, a marathon runner and a good skier, while I was always tense and stiff in a snowplough on the slopes, or panic-stricken if I got out of my depth in the water. But I was changing elsewhere, in different ways, taking on greater responsibilities at work, finding my place in a world where I wasn't defined simply by being a woman, a wife or a mother, and I wasn't just a secretary any more. I worked in budget forecasting in the bookkeeping department, then in HR. Acronyms were used everywhere in EDF. I changed 'SG', service group, progressed up my 'SB', my salary band. As well as being a saint, I was now our safety net.

But I also managed to bring all the different parts of our lives together. My friends were his, and his were mine. We went on holiday with other families. We had parties. We pushed back the furniture at each other's houses and danced the New Year in. At our house, we held parties in the basement, which we had completely done up. We even had a disco ball hanging from the ceiling. Our children were astonished to see their parents acting like teenagers. I remember a long weekend when we went with the children and some other families to Saint-Maximin to stay with Didier, a young engineer who worked at EDF, and his wife in the house they had recently bought. One day Caroline came into the bathroom and found a few of us, including Pascale, in there talking while Didier was brushing his teeth. I was sitting on the toilet. Afterwards Caroline told her father, 'Maman was peeing in front of everybody!' I promised her I hadn't been, the lid was down, I was just sitting on it, that was all. But the image left its mark on her, to the point that twenty years later she asked me again to swear that the lid had been down. What had she felt back then? What was she so afraid of, that she had carried inside herself for so long? Perhaps she thought I had too much self-confidence, too much get-up-and-go, too many friends; perhaps it was the attraction that hovered between Didier and me for years, during a period in which things were more complicated for her father, who was struggling to come to terms with his mother's death.

I was aware of this, but I didn't fully grasp what he was going through. I had lost my mother at the age of nine, and it was hard to understand the sorrow of an adult mourning his mother, having had her in his life for so long. Added to that was the uncertainty of his employment status and his irregular income. Meanwhile I was doing well at EDF and enjoying my job. But for me there was no question of any rivalry, or even climbing the ladder – all I was looking for was stability. What was mine was his. I was pregnant with our third child. Florian was born a few months after Dominique's mother died. He wasn't named after anyone, though it was the name of my hairdresser's son; I simply thought it was beautiful. When Dominique came to see me at the maternity hospital the next day, one of the orderlies said to him, 'You've just missed the father!' Didier had dropped in with a colleague half an hour earlier. A simple misunderstanding. But that sentence would crystallise this fragile moment in Dominique's life, particularly the sense that my world contained more than just him.

I went back to work. The commute seemed endless now that my office had moved to Noisy-le-Grand. More than once, when I finally arrived, I was greeted coldly with the words, 'Have you seen the time?' There was no point telling my boss about the traffic, or the train that had been cancelled, or the fact that my baby hadn't slept. Like all working mothers, I had become a multitasking machine. It was exhausting, but not unmanageable. It wasn't as if I'd ever been led to believe that life was going to be easy.

After a while we began having parties and friends over for dinner again. Pascale told me about an evening when she was slow-dancing with Dominique. As he watched me on the dance floor in Didier's arms, he whispered, 'There's something going on, I don't recognise my wife any more.' He was right. Didier and I had crossed the line a few months after my return from maternity leave. We had become lovers.

With the passing of time, and perhaps even more so in the moment, it's difficult to understand what it is that triggers the beginning of an affair, what makes the brakes and bolts snap. We didn't see each other very often, or at least not very regularly; we met in hotel rooms when he was travelling for work. I discovered a less muscular body, new sensations – not least my first orgasm. In his arms I was no longer the shy little orphan meeting her saviour. No longer the saint my husband reproached me for being. No longer the creature of my obligations. I was about to turn thirty-five, the age my mother was when she died. I thought about this so often. My fear of dying returned, but only for me to overcome it and cry victory. I was going to live longer than she had. I was going to keep my promise. I was going to be happy.

I still loved my husband. I loved both men, I think. I even bought them both the same red jacket. I picked it out for Dominique, and then I got one for Didier too. He didn't exclude the possibility of getting a divorce one day, but not for me. He talked about us as if we were having a secret relationship that might last a lifetime. He even introduced me to his parents as a friend of his. Sometimes I had the impression that I had more in common with him than with my husband, more to talk about, but that was no doubt the privilege of lovers who, for the few hours they have together, feel like they have all the time in the world to talk and make love. One evening in the bathroom at home in Combs-la-Ville, Dominique grabbed me viciously by the collar and screamed that he wanted to know the truth. David and Caroline witnessed the scene. I said nothing. I held strong. 'Admitting it will only hurt other people,' Didier sometimes said. I was lost. One day Pascale saw me burst into tears in the archive-storage room at work. I just didn't know what to do any more. Living a lie had become unbearable. She pressed me to break up with Didier. Dominique had more stature, she said, more confidence. It's funny when I think about it, she put him on a pedestal, but this was before he hit on her and she tried to warn me.

It was around this time that I was offered company housing by EDF, a big house in Gournay-sur-Marne, much closer to work. It would mean selling our home in Combs-la-Ville, the house Dominique had wanted so badly, that we had renovated together, but which marked, as I had feared, the beginning of our financial difficulties. The offer tipped the balance even further to my side, which was strange, all things considered, as if the solution to our problems always came from me – our first little apartment in Brunoy, and now a five-bedroom house. As if everything that Dominique was involved in was doomed to failure.

*

One morning when I was leaving for work he again insisted I tell him the truth. I ended up saying yes, because he was so desperate to know, yes, I was having an affair with Didier. He didn't move, didn't say a word. He was in shock. I left the house. During the day he called me at the office to tell me not to come home. The children were away, staying with his family. I spent the night at Pascale's. The following morning, I woke up with a fever and no voice. Pascale called Dominique to come and fetch me. We left her house and went to pick up the children. David and Florian were staying with his father and Nicole, while Caroline was staying nearby with Pierrette and André, Dominique's half-brother, and her cousins. As soon as we got to his father's house Dominique began drinking. He had got it into his head that I was going to take the children and leave him. The whisky made him increasingly violent. He started insulting me, then grabbed a chair and threatened to smash it over my head. His father was there, as immense and threatening as ever. He tried to reason with Dominique. But he was the role model. It was as if Dominique was turning into one of them, becoming like all the other Pelicot men. In the middle of the night I fled, taking nothing with me, not even my coat, leaving Florian and David. I ran the mile to Pierrette and André's house and when I got there I hid in a cupboard. It was Dominique's brother, Joël, who came to find me. He drove me to Tours and found me a hotel for the night, rather than risk putting me up at his house, and the next day I took the train to Brittany to stay with my father. My stepmother gave me a lecture. How dare I abandon my sons and my daughter? I spared my father the details. He had grown very frail.

Once he had calmed down, Dominique called me. He was back at home with the children, I had to return, we could talk things over. So I went. He told me he had spoken to Didier and asked him what his intentions were towards me. Didier had told him that nothing had happened between us. 'You don't deserve that woman,' Dominique had retorted. I was horribly hurt by Didier's cowardice – not long afterwards he suggested we continue our affair – and I was consumed with guilt towards Dominique. All I read in his violence and anger was the strength of our bond, my transgression and his distress. No one asked me what I wanted; I would have been incapable of answering anyway.

Dominique was becoming sexually demanding again, as if he were regaining exclusive control of my body. I put up with it. I was the one who was at fault. We did end up moving to Gournay-sur-Marne, but I found it enormously difficult to return to our daily life. Florian was three. He had a poor appetite and was a bad sleeper. He dragged his mattress into our bedroom every night. Always on my side. I cuddled him until he went back to sleep, but his anxiety may well have been linked to my unhappiness.

One evening we were invited to a restaurant on the Champs-Elysées to celebrate a property deal that Dominique had been involved in. We needed a babysitter, and he suggested a friend of his called Brigitte. I didn't know her, but I agreed and left him to sort it out. It was his celebration, a rare professional recognition for him. Brigitte didn't look like a babysitter. She was in her forties with a job in a bank, financing property loans, which is how she and Dominique had met. She turned up that evening with her husband. It all seemed a bit odd, but I decided to trust them, and left the house with Dominique. The children were asleep by the time we got back, and Brigitte and her husband left. Not long afterwards I discovered that Dominique had become, or already was, her lover. I didn't say anything, I let it happen. I was still licking my wounds after my break-up with Didier. I wanted Dominique to be happy. In a way, the idea of him having an affair of his own eased my guilt and I imagined it also offered him a more exciting sex life. And that is no doubt why, at the time, I didn't question the fact that he brought his mistress and her husband into our home to look after our children. Now I can't help wondering what kind of twisted scenario he had in mind.

Soon after, he told me he needed time alone to think. He found himself a small apartment in Torcy. I let him go. Perhaps I also needed time apart from him, but I was incapable of putting it into words. I was simply resigned, powerless, I didn't feel like the vivacious woman I'd once been. It made sense that he should seek solace elsewhere. Soon a woman called Michèle, whom he had met while working at a temping agency, moved in with him. I never met her. I accepted that he was happy with another woman. I still loved him, but I didn't want any drama. It wasn't a sacrifice, it was my way of coping. I can fall to pieces over the most trivial thing, but when it comes to what truly matters, I steel myself. I put on a brave face. The children spent time with him at his new place. David was now a young man, embarking on his adult life, and Caroline got on well with her father's new partner. As for Florian – one day, we were all sitting around the kitchen table playing a game where one person would begin a sentence and the next person had to continue it. When it was Florian's turn, he ended the sentence with, 'And I want my daddy!' At the end of six months, Dominique asked me how I was feeling about things. I told him I was ready for him to come home. It was true, I was.

He moved back in. I slowly began to enjoy our life together again. I put my affair with Didier behind me, avoiding him in corridors and the company restaurant. David and Caroline invited friends over; there were always people coming and going, sitting around the table enjoying the meals I loved to cook. But until he was ten, Florian kept up the habit of dragging his mattress into our bedroom, and always on my side. It is possible, despite my precautions, that he heard Dominique and me having sex, as he told the judge at the trial. Even today, he sometimes expresses doubts about his father's identity. I know Dominique is his father, and I've even tried to encourage him to take a DNA test. But perhaps now he prefers to believe that he is not Monsieur Pelicot's son.

Looking back over that whole period, I can't help thinking of the breach it created. I had fallen in love with another man, at the very moment when the death of Dominique's mother had opened up old wounds. Both the women in his life had abandoned him. Perhaps it was then that everything began to go wrong.

During the hearing, Dominique was asked, 'Did your

wife's extramarital affair change something in you?' No, he replied. And it's true that afterwards we had almost laughed about it. We were relieved to be back together. We had met when we were so young, we had no experience — that was what we said to erase the whole business. We laughed at the kids we had once been. We had lost our innocence.

But the little flame was still there. Impossible to extinguish. To some my faith in our relationship will look like weakness now that we know how the story ends. But the more I think about it, the more I try to piece it all together, the more certain I become that he could have taken more partners, had more experiences, sated his sexual appetite elsewhere. He could have left me for good, but deep down that was impossible for him. Our meeting had signalled the end of the nightmare, as he once wrote. It was the key to his existence. What mattered was that he possessed me.

NINE

By the time Christmas arrived our family had disintegrated. We didn't spend Christmas Eve together. The horror was etched deep in each of us. I spent the evening at Florian's house, with him, his partner, Aurore, who was pregnant with their third child, and their two daughters, Ella and Anna. We had champagne and foie gras and tried to pretend everything was normal. It's strange to think that we managed it somehow – we got dressed up and clinked glasses while we were devastated inside. I couldn't stop thinking of all those who were absent.

Earlier in the evening there had been a discreet knock at the door. It was my grandson Maxime, and behind him, Caroline. He rushed towards me holding out a gift. I unwrapped it and found a lovely necklace with a blue stone, chosen by his mother. She was expressing her generosity to me through her son. I was touched. But she stayed outside on the doorstep and refused to come in. She was furious with her brother for having put me up, for having made it possible for me to leave her house, and she was furious with me for not staying. I could hear the anger in her voice as she spoke to Florian outside. I stayed back.

Knowing that she was standing outside reminded me of

other sad Christmases. The one we celebrated in an empty living room in Gournay-sur-Marne after all our furniture had been repossessed. David was fifteen, Caroline eleven, and Florian four. We ate dinner on the garden furniture that the bailiffs had left behind. As if to ward off bad luck, Dominique gave me a ring. I didn't want it. It wasn't the right time for such an extravagant gift, especially after I had been so careful not to spend too much on the children. I stood up from the table, went into the kitchen and burst into tears. Caroline came after me and shouted at me for hurting her father's feelings. She'd felt the same need as I'd always had to protect him.

Her current distress was no doubt a reflection of how close they had been when she was little. I wanted to help her now, but I didn't know what to do or how to reach her in those moments. I was feeling extremely fragile myself, even if I did my best not to show it. I embraced silence; she demanded noise. I clung to the presence of my grandson beside me. His birth had brought Caroline and me closer; I remember how much she'd wanted to have a child, how long she'd had to wait, and then the surprise she put on my plate during a family lunch. 'Look under the napkin!' she urged me. I was thrilled and deeply moved to find the blurry image of an ultrasound. Eventually, to our great joy, Maxime was born.

And here he was now, standing before me, upset by the abrupt dissolution of all our family rituals, prisoner of a conflict of loyalty between his mother, waiting for him outside, and his grandmother, who had looked after him so often, with whom he had spent so much time. I knew his habits, his tastes, his form teacher, his friends, his schoolbooks, and now all of a sudden we were only allowed a few minutes together on Christmas Eve. But he didn't let his feelings show. I wished I could have given him a present, but I wasn't expecting to see him, and in any case I hadn't had the energy to do any Christmas shopping. I simply transferred some money to my three children's bank accounts so they could buy gifts for my grandchildren from me. I gave Maxime a hug so he could go back to his mother, and they left. The following day, I called David and invited myself over. It was Christmas Day and it had always been at his and Céline's house that the family came together to celebrate birthdays and holidays. He is so gregarious, he always loved the gatherings and parties we held when he was a child, just as he liked to make people laugh at school. He has a generosity, a need to be surrounded by people. And yet I sensed a certain coolness in his voice.

'Why don't you drop by for dessert?' he said.

He was the one to open the front door. Céline came to say hello. I could hear Caroline and Pierre's voices coming from the dining room and the children's from the living room. I went straight into the living room to see my grandchildren. I wanted a little of the joy and sweetness that this special day held for the children. How much did they understand of what was going on?

Only the eldest, Nathan, had been given something like an explanation. He was fourteen. They told him that his grandfather had raped his grandmother and was in prison. I don't know what he made of this. Nor what his sisters, Charlize and

Clémence, had heard. All they had said to me a few weeks earlier was, 'What a pity we won't come to swim in the pool in Mazan any more.'

'There'll be other holidays,' I had promised, without knowing where or when.

That Christmas Day we talked about other things. Maxime was happy to spend a few more hours with me.

From the doorway, Caroline and Pierre beckoned to him that it was time to leave. They didn't come in to talk to me, and I didn't go out to them. We were a broken family now, our raw emotions exposing old rivalries from their childhood. Caroline was angry with me for having chosen to stay with her younger brother. David was angry that it was Florian who had gone down with me when I cleared out the house in Mazan. They both wanted to be there for me, to protect me in their own way. But I felt as if they wanted to take possession of my life. I couldn't bear that. I didn't want to be dependent on them. How could I explain to them that I needed time on my own?

I had been by myself for the last few days. Pascale was on holiday in the Antilles for a fortnight, and had left me the keys to her apartment while she was away. It was on the fifth floor of a modern building near the Porte de Versailles in Paris. It felt good to be staying in a friend's apartment, a woman who was single, had no children, took care of herself and of her home – exactly the set-up I was heading towards. I was sixty-eight and alone for the first time in my life.

On New Year's Eve, as 2021 bade good riddance to 2020, to Doumé and Mino, it also bade farewell to happy times, and to our house in Provence, whose entire contents were now up for sale online. I had no idea what the future held. I navigated the storm with no one to talk to but myself and my dog. And that was exactly what I wanted. Around midnight I received a message from Caroline; she said that she loved me, I meant the world to her, and I mustn't do anything silly. She had found out that I was alone at Pascale's and thought I might jump from the fifth floor. But that isn't me. I am the enemy of death, it has taken too much from me. I told her not to worry, that I loved her too, and wished her a happy New Year. I spent the evening binge-watching all the episodes of *The Queen's Gambit*, the hit American series about a rebellious orphan girl who becomes a chess grandmaster. I stayed up until five in the morning, my orphan's eyes wide open.

I returned to Florian's house after Pascale came back from her holiday. But she carried on helping me with everything I had to do. There was something restorative about doing it all with her, whereas with my children it would have been more painful. A role reversal I could not bear. They had their lives, I had mine. Female friendship made this difficult period of my life easier; it was like rediscovering the closeness of young girls sighing and dreaming together, wondering what the future might hold. We were just a few years further along the road, after the delusions of marriage. We laughed at seemingly fateful coincidences: a woman called Madame Toupris – Mrs Takeall – who was dealing with my tax affairs, Madame Pardon who set up the debt management plan in my name. Pascale lent me a bit of money to tide me over. She suggested I apply for social housing, which I did with little enthusiasm – I wasn't sure I wanted to come back to live in the Paris region. The urban hellscape that surrounded her apartment by the Porte de Versailles, with its tangle of avenues, tunnels and junctions alongside the ring road, made me nostalgic for the Provence countryside. Where should I go? I had no ties. It felt as if all the landscapes I had known throughout my life, from Germany to Provence, were stage sets that vanished as soon as I left. I was inhabiting an old wound. The path ahead was about closing it, healing it. Pascale was surprised one day to hear me say that I hoped I might fall in love again. She couldn't get over the fact that I hadn't sworn off men for good. So many women our age were doing precisely that, with a mix of bitterness and relief.

I had an appointment on January 21st with the court-appointed expert psychologist. He had a slew of questions for me. I told him about my mother's death, my father the soldier and his absences, my maternal grandmother's affection and natural authority, my sour stepmother, her daughter, the lack of love, my perfect scores in dictation, how I left school very young, my early sexual experiences with Dominique, his demands, our children. At the end he passed me a blank sheet of paper and asked me to sign it, which I did on the bottom right-hand corner, mechanically. 'You are a subjugated woman, under your husband's control,' he concluded. 'His little slave girl.'

But the master does not put his slave girl to sleep in order to have her at his mercy! He commands and watches her suffer. What could he know about me, about us, about our love? Nothing! I had never been Dominique's slave. And he had not always been my tormentor. That was not the man I had married. I left the consulting room in a rage. There were so many versions of our story now. Those of the children, the police and the expert witnesses. In other people's eyes, mine was crumbling.

Yet I still clung to it. I tried to understand. Just to understand. I didn't deny the crime, even though I didn't yet have the strength to find out the details or the extent of it. I was willing to answer questions, even the most intimate ones. But I didn't recognise my life as it was summed up by other people. I had been happy, I was sure of it. I was more than just a victim.

I went down to Mazan and cleaned the house from top to bottom, hoping to get back the deposit. The landlady was not interested in doing me any favours. Whatever hadn't sold – the coffee table, the wall-mounted television in our bedroom – was given to charity. Les Restos du Cœur, an organisation that gives meals to people in need, bought Dominique's car for a token sum. I gave back the keys to the house.

I returned to the Le Pontet prison with a blouson jacket and a few other things for Dominique. Sylvie came with me. We sat on a bench outside while we waited for visiting hours to begin, watching as other people, mostly women, arrived to see their husbands, brothers or sons. With my bag of winter clothes, I must have seemed like one of them. I looked exactly as you would expect a supportive wife or mother to look. Except that I was also the victim.

Even Dominique didn't expect this much from me. The first time I'd been to drop off clothes with Florian, he wrote to Michel, Sylvie's husband, to thank him. He had imagined some sort of male solidarity. 'I think it must have been you, Michel, who sent me warm clothes that reminded me of the smell of home. I found a hair from the love of my life that warmed my heart for a brief moment.'

No, it was me who was still worrying that he might be cold. It was me, the love of his life whom he had raped, whose body he had served up to criminals. Me, whose every single hair bore the trace of his poisons. Sylvie told me about the letter and sent it on to me. Florian and I read it together. We both cried. Dominique sounded as if he were worried about threats of possible attacks within the prison. Inside, sex offenders deserve special punishment.

In a subsequent letter to some friends from Mazan he talked about a fellow inmate who no longer wanted to share a cell with him once he found out what he had done. Dominique even accused Caroline of talking to the man's family. I called Caroline and asked her if this was true. She was appalled that I could believe such a thing, and she was right, Dominique was manipulating us. He was using prison rumours to deepen the rifts between us, to rub salt in our open wounds. After betraying and breaking us, Dominique still managed to torment us, and somehow I still believed him.

The imposing prison door swung open and the visitors filed into the building to see their loved ones. I handed the bag of warm clothes to the guard at reception and we left.

During this time the case had been transferred from the team at Carpentras to the criminal-investigation unit of the Avignon police, who were painstakingly working to identify and track down one by one each of the men who had come to the house to rape me, breaking their aliases on the dark web that shelters creeps and perverts, finding their addresses, knocking at their doors. Many had wives and children. Men of all ages and occupations, the kinds of men you come across all the time, were now in custody, most of them insisting they had done nothing wrong. The transcripts of their interrogations had been added to the case file to which our lawyer had access. She read them aloud to me, as she had at our meeting with Caroline and David. I listened, paralysed, to the accounts of what the men had done to me, nothing of which I had any recollection of. The description in words of the videos I refused to watch. 'Say something! Why don't you say something?' Caroline cried. Our lawyer reminded her that everyone deals with things in their own way, and at the end of the meeting she told us that she would no longer see us together. She sometimes called me to tell me about another arrest or to read out the latest confession. She added her own coarse, even crude, comments as if we were old friends, or some kind of commando taking revenge on the filthy bastards who had used me like a blow-up doll. The plain-speaking camaraderie that had marked our relationship from the start was becoming unbearable. I wished she would filter her words, protect me from them, leave me to feel my way forward at my own pace. I still refused to watch the videos. But I was slowly and painfully integrating the knowledge of who my husband really was and what he had done to me.

'Open your eyes, Maman! Look what he did to you!' the children kept repeating.

By then, I had been living with Aurore and Florian for a few months. My relationship with Florian was calm. He respected my thought process. Strangely enough, it was this child – born during the most fragile moment in our marriage – who now seemed to understand me best. He had no trouble grasping the facts; he even realised, with some bitterness, that the warning signs had been there all along, though he couldn't possibly have deciphered them at the time.

Aurore gave a statement to the police in March 2021. She recalled an incident she had never spoken of before: she once thought she overheard Dominique saying that he wanted to 'play doctor' with Nathan. Those words had resonated in her mind, she told the investigators, because at the time she herself was involved in proceedings against her grandfather, who had abused her. But the resonance was so strong that she had feared mixing everything up, misinterpreting what she had heard. She told Florian, and together they decided not to say anything. Confronted now with the gravity of the charges against Dominique, that distant memory resurfaced.

A month later, Aurore's statement was read aloud to us by our lawyer in her office. I was with Caroline and David. David asked her to read that passage again – it concerned his son, who would have been three years old at the time.

In the car afterwards, David was livid. To learn all this so many years later – and through a report rather than from Aurore or his brother. And he was worried. We knew the grandchildren were already suffering. Our initial precautions had quickly fallen away. Our anxiety, our adult words, had spilled over. Even our silences betrayed us. It had been impossible to protect the children. They were caught in the shockwave – the family cataclysm Dominique had unleashed. I often wondered how the children would grow, whether I would know how to reassure them.

I asked Céline if I could speak to Nathan. She encouraged me to. I went up to his room and told him that if he needed to talk about anything, if he had questions, I was there. He didn't really know what to say – which was perfectly understandable. It was heartbreaking to impose on him such a collapse of his bearings, a family ordeal at an age when you're searching for yourself, stepping down that long, knotty passage towards adulthood – and the time of first loves too.

His answers were the short ones teenagers give: yeah, no, I dunno. It isn't easy to gather a fifteen-year-old boy into your arms. I kept telling him not to worry, that we would get through this, that I would hold on and that things would be all right for him too, that he could count on me, on all of us. I told him how happy I had been to watch him be born and grow.

I knew perfectly well that all the sweet moments in life weigh very little against horrors like these once they come to light – that those happy memories might even seem suspect, absurd or false. But they were all I had, for myself and for them. When I reminded David how close he had been to his father, how Dominique had always been there for him, helping him at every stage of his life, it only fed his rage. We were both watching our lives ebb away, each on a different bank. I was upstream; he was downstream.

In the days that followed, David had a violent argument with Florian about Aurore's statement. He reproached him for keeping everything to himself for years, without thinking of Nathan – of any of them. Florian was devastated and blamed himself. The bond between my sons was breaking; my family was disintegrating further.

I returned to my impossible puzzle. I plunged back in time, to the years when I was still working, when Dominique sometimes looked after Nathan at our home in Noisy-le-Grand. Never had I seen our grandson pull away from him or show any distrust. I clung to my memories while David and Céline sifted through theirs.

Eventually they told Nathan what his Aunt Aurore had reported to the police. He had been seeing a psychologist since November 2020. I had no idea how to help him myself – I couldn't find the words – and it hurt to watch him forced to search his own memory in turn.

Since learning what his grandfather had done to me, he had spoken, mostly to his mother, about a recurring nightmare. One evening, when we were having dinner at Caroline and Pierre's, he brought it up. I told Nathan that a dream isn't a fact, that one has to be careful not to treat it as a true, precise memory. I wanted him to move forward, to stay afloat. I know all too well the devastation sadness can bring; I had watched it consume my brother. Nathan was only fifteen at the time. David abruptly cut the conversation short. Our wounds were bleeding more and more.

'Maman, you have to look at your case file,' Caroline said. She was more familiar with it than me, it was true. Caroline had spent hours delving into its pages, looking at the photos of her mother being raped, symbolically killed. I was very upset when I found out. It was not going to quell my daughter's anger. Especially as Dominique's brother, Joël, with all his medical authority, had assured her that her father had almost certainly raped her too. Caroline and I have spoken numerous times about the two photos taken in the dark. We have tried to work out when and where it was – surely sometime in the last ten years. Caroline originally thought it was our house in Villiers-sur-Marne, but the colour of the sheets made me think they were more likely taken at her house. It is unbearable to imagine her father looking at her in that incestuous way in her own home. I kept trying to reassure her that it was implausible that he had raped her, she was asleep in bed with her husband, and Dominique never went over there without me. I wasn't trying to defend him, I wanted to help my daughter, and could see no other way of doing so except by going through all the places and dates we had spent time all together, so as not to allow doubt and suspicion to poison her.

I already did a lot of walking in the countryside around Mazan, and I got back into it while I was staying with David. I began going off on my own for three or four hours at a time with our two dogs. These long spells alone were good for me. They were healing. I was not turning away from the horror, I was pitting myself against it with my tears, my solitude, my sorrow and my happy memories. I partitioned Dominique into two, the same way I somehow managed to separate my violated body from my sense of self. I was not protecting him, I was protecting myself. That was how I was slowly able to begin the process of mourning, something that anger would not have allowed. Anger, for me, blocks everything: thoughts, emotions, any possibility of solace.

May 31st 2021 was the day of the first mediation session for our divorce proceedings. I would have liked to be in the same room as Dominique, but I took my seat in the courtroom in Carpentras, accompanied by a family law specialist recommended by my lawyer, facing the family court judge, while Dominique was in Marseille, having been transferred to Les Baumettes prison. The meeting was conducted by video link. Next to Dominique sat his lawyer, a petite woman with short hair and round glasses called Béatrice Zavarro. The microphones had not yet been switched on. I had to turn my head to look at him on the screen. I was seeing him for the first time since I had watched him walk up the staircase inside Carpentras police station. His eyes were lowered. Avoiding mine. I thought he seemed terribly thin. He wore a brace on his left shoulder.

We were both asked to leave the room so the lawyers could talk among themselves for a few minutes. When I came back in, the microphones had been turned on. Seven months since I'd heard the sound of his voice. He told me he was sorry. Asked me to forgive him. I told him I wanted a divorce.

As the session drew to a close, I asked if I could speak to him directly. I needed to talk to him. The judge was sympathetic. The lawyers left the room and she stayed. I stood up to face the screen. I told him Florian and Aurore had a new baby boy called Charlie.

'What a strange name,' he said.

I asked him why he was wearing a shoulder brace. He told me that being handcuffed with his hands behind his back had aggravated the inflammation in his shoulder, and he had been granted his request to be handcuffed in front from now on. I asked why he had a plaster on his cheek. He told me there had been a brawl in the prison courtyard and he had come to the defence of another inmate. In other words I began by asking for his news. 'You're his best advocate,' my lawyer often berated me. I believed he belonged in prison, but I would not kick a man when he was down.

Later, when she called me to discuss the details of the divorce and suggested a significant sum of money in compensation, I told her I didn't want any money, and, anyway, Dominique was broke. She insisted. I ended up agreeing to a request for a symbolic payment of one euro. She asked me if I believed in God. I said, 'No, I believe in forces that are bigger than us, but not in a God.' I like going into a church when there is no Mass being held. I go in for the silence and to light candles. I had nothing to demand from Dominique after the fifty years I had spent with him. Only explanations and a divorce. I was reverting to my father's surname. Gisèle Guillou.

TEN

I began taking sleeping pills after my father died in December 1992. I'd stopped sleeping. I was prescribed zolpidem, the same medication I found years later recorded on the charge sheet: 'lorazepam & zolpidem'. The ingredients of chemical submission. 'Whatever you do, don't give her more than eight grammes, you could kill her,' a male nurse who was active on a perverts' website warned Dominique.

After Papa died it was just a quarter of a zolpidem pill, which I took only very occasionally. It didn't really work for me anyway. I preferred the radio to lull me to sleep. I still do. I've had trouble sleeping since my father passed away.

I had just turned forty. For my birthday he had slipped me an envelope containing some money. 'It's for you.' Furtively, behind my stepmother's back, as always. Like the time I went to visit him with Florian, who was then four. I wanted grandfather and grandson to at least have met, even if they couldn't really get to know each other properly. My father's health was declining rapidly and I felt time was running out. As Florian and I were leaving, my father was adamant that we go together to check the tyre pressure on my car. My stepmother muttered that I was old enough to do it alone, but he insisted. It was a ploy; he took advantage of the outing to withdraw some money, which he popped into an envelope and handed me with his still-functioning arm. 'This is for you and the little ones.'

I would have loved for my children to have got to know him better, to have been able to spend more time with this gentle, kind man, but between his health problems and my stepmother's meanness I was never able to leave the children with them. How I wish that he had not been forced to hide the fact that he wanted to give his daughter a gift to help her out a little, that he might have raised his voice occasionally to challenge his wife, but he never had and he never would, as if he knew that any resistance was futile. I figured this out when I was very young.

Maybe it was that summer evening when we were on holiday in Brittany, the two of them sitting on their double bed, in the same room where Michel and I were sleeping on the opened-out sofa. I don't think our presence stole a second away from their intimacy. 'Life's a shit sandwich, and you take a little bite of it every day,' my stepmother declared. There was a long silence. I would have been twelve or thirteen. Was I the only one to rebel inwardly against this fatalistic attitude? Earlier that day I had been filled with joy as I ran along the beach in Névez in my bathing suit – a beach so beautiful, with its turquoise waters and expanse of fine white sand, that everyone calls it Tahiti. Even if only for those few moments, life was to be savoured, like the pain au chocolat we gobbled down every afternoon. I wanted to keep my hymn to life inside me. But my brother, lying beside me, didn't move, perhaps already inclined to believe that she was right. My father didn't say anything either. Misfortune pursued him, and he had decided to marry it.

    He was one of those men who withdraw into themselves as they age, who don't even try to exercise the authority of a husband or father that the world bestows on them. They leave that to others. Papa bore the scars of too many wounds to be able to disguise them. When he was alone he liked to listen to classical music with the volume turned up. I do too. Like him, I let Mozart express a part of me that I keep hidden. I have a framed photo of my father hung in the entrance of my house. He is in his fifties, sitting in profile in front of a window, wearing a white shirt, tie and cufflinks. It must have been taken during a family lunch. It is difficult to see his expression: his eyes are raised to the sky and the horizon, and he is looking away from the camera just as he is in that other photograph taken with Maman on his arm in a Paris street when he was on leave. Deep down he had always been no more than a shadow of himself. His eyes expressed this, his body too – a body that had survived bloody wars but had been eaten away from the inside, first by a perforated ulcer, then hemiplegia on the right side, and eventually terminal stomach cancer.

As his condition deteriorated, I took to visiting him in Brittany more frequently. His life was ebbing away, he no longer talked to me only about Maman but also about his own mother, who had died when he was seven. I told him she was waiting for him somewhere at the end of the tunnel, that he would find her there, bathed in beautiful light. These were not hollow words. We were father and daughter, and we had both lost our mothers when we were much too young.

He went into hospital on a Tuesday. As soon as I heard, I set about organising things at work and for the children, so that I could leave on Friday morning. I wanted to see the doctors before the hospital corridors emptied for the weekend. Papa lay there, painfully thin on his hospital bed. He was just skin and bone. He had a raging fever. He said that the walls of the room were closing in on him. I managed to speak to a doctor alone. I can still see him as if it were yesterday, pointing out on a scan where the cancer had metastasised all over my father's body. I remember how he didn't mince his words. 'It's all over,' he said. I asked how much longer he had. A few hours, maybe a week or two, he replied. I stayed until Sunday. My stepmother didn't let us have a single minute alone. She knew only too well the circle we would form in her absence, the memories and the ghosts we would conjure up. On Sunday afternoon, December 13th 1992, I had to leave. I was working the next day. I wanted to weep, but not in front of her, and I didn't want it to seem like I was saying a final goodbye. 'I'll be back,' I promised. Papa saw my red eyes. 'I love you, my darling,' he said. I knew he was proud of me, that I reminded him of Maman, of her smile. I had kept my promise. My train was at 6.30 that evening. It was dark when I left. I remember looking at my watch an hour into the journey, the very moment that Papa passed away.

He had planned his funeral down to the last detail. He wanted to be buried where he was born, in Scaër, with his brothers. There was a place for his second wife too. He would wear his military medals. It was what he wanted. There was a great turnout. He had been a faithful supporter of the town's youth football club, and in his later years he had also taken to helping local people deal with bureaucratic issues. Right up until his death, he had focused on doing his duty. But I knew he had originally dreamed of being buried next to Maman in Azay-le-Ferron. That spot ended up being for my brother, Michel.

Michel stood alongside me at the funeral. Silent. Closed. For a long time I had watched him falling apart, as he desperately searched for some meaning to his life. When he was young he used to come and see us in Brunoy. Dominique always tried to put a smile back on his face. Because Michel was so unhappy working on building sites, I suggested he apply for the selection process for the Post, Telegram and Telephone service. He got a job on the post train, sorting letters and travelling around the country. But when he was thirty he fell into a severe depression. He called me from the Pitié-Salpêtrière hospital in Paris and I hurried to his bedside. From being the younger married sister with two children, I became a kind of familial authority. The psychiatrist was very concerned, and asked me to tell my father to come and see his son. When I phoned it was my stepmother who answered. 'Do you want to finish him off? Don't you dare speak to your father about this,' she said. Stupidly, I obeyed.

It was Aunt Louisette who ended up telling him. She had kept an eye on us ever since we were schoolchildren in Paris. Papa was obviously upset that I hadn't said anything to him. 'How could you hide such a thing from me?' he snapped at me over the phone. I didn't dare tell him that it was his wife who had insisted. I protected her. I wanted to protect everybody.

It was during this time that Michel confided in me, 'If anything happens to me I want to be buried with Maman.' When he came out of hospital, he went off with the young man with whom he shared a room; they moved in with the young man's mother. My father visited him there. He was worried. Michel was turning in on himself. Our phone calls became less frequent. I don't know what the nature of their relationship was. Sometimes I wondered if they were in love, if my brother was in love with a man, afraid of being judged, but he was extremely discreet, and I could have been wrong. I respected his silence. I saw him at our father's funeral, and because it was a couple of weeks before Christmas, he spent the holidays with us. The children gave their sad uncle a pair of braces.

He died less than two years later, on July 2nd 1994. That day, strangely enough, I was out buying flowers to take to a dinner party, and I wandered into a shop that makes wreaths for funerals near Place de la Nation in Paris. As soon as I realised it wasn't an ordinary florist, I apologised and turned to leave, but the saleswoman insisted on making up a bouquet for me: it would make a nice change from the dead. I had no idea that Michel had just suffered a heart attack on the train to the Pyrenees and had passed away to the sound of the siren in the ambulance transporting him to the hospital in Orléans. I asked her for roses, baby's breath and cornflowers.

We were only informed two days later. Dominique and I went straight down to Orléans. As she led us to the morgue in the hospital basement, a nurse warned me not to go in and see the body; it had become cyanotic. It had turned so blue, it was almost black. But he had to be formally identified. Dominique offered to do it for me. He returned in a state of shock. Michel was forty-three years old.

He was buried next to Maman, as he had wished, under the same grey granite headstone, in the cemetery of Azay-le-Ferron. His colleagues in the railways later placed a plaque on the gravestone, etched with a train and a message of fond memories: 'Here lie Jeanne Gillou, née Prot (1926–1962), and her son, Michel (1951–1994).'

I was forty-two and the only one left. I couldn't sleep. And indeed I would never again, or only very rarely, experience the kind of deep, untroubled sleep that carries you straight through to morning. Still, grief did not get the better of me. That must be why our money worries, our infidelities, all the issues that had erupted in recent years, seemed bearable. We were still on the side of life, with all its ups and downs.

I bought myself a suede coat with a fur lining that I found in a boutique called Mac Douglas. I only dared set foot in there thanks to the money my father had given me for my fortieth birthday. For you, he'd said. Just for me, for once. Though our financial situation was extremely tight, I decided to treat myself. That beautiful coat earned me many compliments. People told me how elegant I looked. It was a gift from my father worn over my old familiar suit of armour.

*

At the foot of the bed in our room stood a valet stand on which Dominique would hang his suit jacket, trousers and waistcoat, which sometimes went unworn for months. He was often out of a job. He had worked for several estate agents, but his foray into property had not been particularly successful. He spent most of his days at home. But he didn't mope. He had DIY projects; he cooked, treating us to chocolate ganache desserts and home-made yoghurt; he did the ironing; he picked Florian up from school, dropped Caroline off at dance class, and made the most of this free time to share with David a passion for action films. By the time I got home from work, everything was ready. This role reversal seemed to amuse him as much as me. Our life was so far removed from the traditions and strictures that had stifled our parents. So far removed from the terrifying father figure who had devastated his childhood. The past could not catch up with us.

And the world was changing so fast, including the working world. Computing was everywhere and I was a part of it, regularly attending training courses through my job. I was promoted. I left the bookkeeping department for HR, where I dealt with Employment Solidarity Contracts, a system of state-subsidised contracts to facilitate the reintegration of the unemployed into working life. I had become part of the bourgeoisie. I wasn't aware of it – there were still so many tiny humiliations, old wounds and lingering insecurities festering inside me – but on the outside and in other people's eyes, both at work and at home, that's how it seemed. It's strange now that I think of it: Dominique should have been the one working for EDF, he was the electrician after all.

Fortunately, his spells of unemployment never lasted too long. One of our neighbours got him a job with the telephone company where he worked. Dominique became a commercial technician. He started wearing a suit again. And he began getting home later than me again, dropping his briefcase in the hallway and coming to join me in the kitchen while I was preparing dinner.

Outside the window, the laurel hedges and flower beds filled with geraniums were some of the most beautiful on our street, allée Auguste Renoir in Gournay-sur-Marne. I only needed to glance at them to feel a sense of safety. There were no dangers lurking on the quiet streets where our children grew up popping in and out of their friends' houses. We called the neighbourhood Meeker Village, after the property developer who built it. Like so many others, Meeker had spotted the investment potential of a booming Parisian suburb, but for us it was as if a new frontier had been drawn, as if we had been gifted bedrooms with en-suite bathrooms, quiet, space and sunlight, a blank page on which to write our story. We associated the Meeker logo with our well-being, just as our Carrefour credit card provided for all our needs and desires. It allowed us to take out loans to go on holidays much further afield than our native Indre – to Spain or the Ermioni Aquarius Club in Greece – and it also came in handy when it was time to pay the monthly fees for the private school where we'd enrolled David after he'd fallen seriously behind, with the hope that he would pass the school certificate at the age of fifteen. Concerned by the poor reputation of the local state school, we ended up enrolling Caroline and Florian in the same private school when they were sixteen. It wasn't a huge amount of money, and we wanted our children to go to university, as we had not. We wanted them to have the opposite of the environment we had grown up in, the opposite of the hardship we had known.

We were heading straight for the day when all our things would be repossessed before Caroline's terrified eyes, and that pitiful Christmas at the garden table. Added to this was a five-year period of deductions to my salary, because after my father died I had to pay inheritance tax on his estate for myself and for my brother who had died after him, and I didn't have the money to pay it all at once. Meanwhile, a tax adviser suggested a sham divorce so that my salary, which was higher than my husband's, and, unlike his, came in regularly, would not be siphoned off to pay all our debts. I thought the idea was totally mad, absolutely out of the question. I wanted nothing to do with it.

Our marital crises were a thing of the past. As far as our sex life was concerned, nothing suggested twenty years of marriage and three children; we felt none of the boredom and friction that slowly wear couples down and make them turn their backs on each other when they go to bed at night. I might sometimes have been happy just to lay my head on Dominique's chest and let my fatigue dissipate, but he was still very demanding sexually, so I allowed myself to be carried away. I sometimes even felt desire. I had set my boundaries and he always respected them, though he still teased me that

I was a saint, which coming from him never sounded like a compliment. He repeated it often, yet I never suspected any dangerous impulse lurking under his skull, nor imagined the line between good and evil being crossed. I used to tease him back, quite calmly, the way old couples repeat themselves, that he should find a woman who was more his type, less shy, less reserved than me. We could speak to each other like that; our respective affairs had made such conversations possible. But he invariably replied, 'No, it's you I want.'

I was taken aback the first time he called me 'my bitch' or 'my little bitch' when we were making love. I yelled at him, but it was a game of his; it turned him on, like an old cliché of erotic literature or pornography. In Gérard de Villiers' spy novels, whose yellowing spines could be found on bookshelves all over France, almost all the women were bitches. I preferred it when he called me 'my little painter', because sometimes during the day, particularly when I was tidying the house, chasing away mess and dust, I'd whistle to myself, like an artist whistling while he worked, as though to convince myself that all was well, after all we'd been through. And yet I knew that clean, fragrant houses have a way of summoning bad news; the thought came back to me often, carried by the scents of Miror brass polish and beeswax, by the memory of a chicken being plucked for a good meal, by my cousin Micheline being burnt and my mother lying stretched out in the kitchen.

Twice, during the 1990s, Dominique came home in tears. He told me he had lost his job. Both times I set his mind at rest. We'd get through. And eventually another job came along. He was building up a whole network of connections that allowed him to bounce back. The telecoms industry was rapidly expanding, and people were gradually getting used to having a mobile phone glued to the palm of their hand. Dominique specialised in strong currents and weak currents, as they're known in electrical jargon – such telling words! Was this man with an erratic professional life strong or weak? Did he sense himself becoming like his father, going from one job to another, never satisfied and never satisfying anyone?

At the time, I didn't make the connection. Life was about making it through to the next day. It was about getting used to the idea that David didn't like school. Helping him find his first job, which Dominique did by introducing him to the world of property. It was about getting used to the idea of upsetting Caroline, who'd always been a good student, but hadn't worked hard enough in Year 10 to get into a mainstream lycée, and would have to go to a vocational school instead. I made her repeat the year so she could get the results required to get into the lycée, told her she had to go to university, get a good job of her choosing and become an independent woman. The words I said to her I had never heard said to me. Our life now was the complete opposite to how mine had been at her age. It was about going with my daughter to her first appointment with the gynaecologist. It was about a shared confidence one morning in the bathroom when she was a teenager. 'I can understand why you had an affair,' she said, 'otherwise you'd only have had Papa in your life.' But the tensions kept returning. I blamed them on adolescence; others said it was the inevitable turbulence between mothers and daughters. I didn't know. No mother, no woman, had ever guided me. I had never opposed anyone. Caroline's outbursts sometimes brought me to the edge of tears.

Life was so busy we barely had time to think. Florian was growing up but he still kept dragging his mattress into our bedroom next to my side of the bed. And I finally realised that he had somehow contrived to repeat Year 5, because moving into Year 6 meant going on the school skiing trip and being apart from me. Did he sense, deep down, that it was possible to lose one's mother at the age of nine? Were our past tragedies coming back to haunt our children?

Those questions are only emerging now. Back then they were very remote. The whole point was that our family was supposed to be healing us. It was a rampart against the violence of our own childhoods, and against our children's fears. We wanted to be with them, to stand by them, deluded enough to believe that anything and everything could somehow be sorted out. When Caroline told us a few years later that she wanted to earn a bit of money while she was studying, Dominique found her some part-time work cleaning the offices of an estate agent friend in Torcy. And then, when she was snowed under with work for her finals, it was her father and I who went every Sunday evening at seven o'clock to do the cleaning in her place. We would tear ourselves away from our Sunday rest to dust and vacuum the premises and take out the bins. But it was important: this way Caroline would keep getting a payslip. We were slaves not so much to our children as to our own painful memories. Perhaps it amounts to the same thing.

For them as well as for us we continued to take out loans, to nudge up the credit limit of our Carrefour card and fulfil our longing for new things: nothing lavish, just little treats, new clothes we liked, that sort of thing. We never dreamed of being rich, just comfortable. But with an interest rate approaching twenty per cent, paying off our debts soon became impossible. So when in 1999 the idea of divorce came up again as a way of ring-fencing my salary, we decided to do it. We appeared before the judge, a woman, who seemed surprised that I wasn't asking for more, for some kind of compensatory payment. She was clearly on my side and would have liked me to be more aggressive. I had taken on a lawyer who knew what we were doing. He advised me to pretend we were genuinely getting divorced. I told the judge I was happy with our amicable agreement, and I wanted things to move ahead quickly. When we finally left we were careful not to let it show we were both in on it. We were no longer officially husband and wife in the eyes of the law, but what did that matter, since we were still together?

The armoured tanks in my nightmares withdrew, but another recurring dream took their place. Two men entered the house. I hid beneath my bed. I saw their feet pacing around the room as they searched for me. There was nothing to understand.

ELEVEN

Our lawyer warned me that journalists had been calling her as the media seized on the story. She explained that the identities of victims of sexual assault were protected and asked what name I would prefer to appear under – it was now just a question of when the first article would appear. Marie, I said. My middle name, and the name of my maternal grandmother, the strongest woman I have ever known, upright in her mourning dress. She always used to say that carnations bring bad luck. She was right. Dominique had worn one in his buttonhole the day of our wedding.

The news broke on October 6th 2021. A friend called to warn me. The banner on the front cover of *Le Nouveau Détective*, a weekly true-crime magazine, read, 'Revealed: The worst case ever. For ten years, he drugged his wife to offer her to other men. THE VAUCLUSE RAPIST NETWORK.' A few lines dragging our life through the mud, just beneath the face of a notorious serial killer. The story was catnip for the lurid tabloid newspapers at the backs of news-stands and the posters in the windows of bar-tobacconists. They have no merit apart from reminding us that there is no hell except on earth. I went to buy a copy.

Inside the magazine, Dominique's blurred face took my

breath away. I recognised the image straight away, without knowing how it had ended up there; I had taken that picture of him on the beach with our grandson while we were looking after him during the school holidays. That day, I had thought I was immortalising what I held most dear. I could just about make out the hair on the top of Maxime's head beneath his grandfather's chin in the crudely cropped picture. Everything else turned to dust: our bond, our love, our walks along the beach. Our memories had been put through a shredder that spat out nothing but a smiling criminal.

They called him Dominique P., 'a sixty-something retired tradesman, married to the victim for half a century'. I, therefore, was Marie P. 'Dominique P. is outgoing, demonstrative even,' according to the magazine. 'Marie, a slight woman of sixty-five, is gentle, almost timid.' Everything was in place for a drama of domination to unfold. Even our bulldog had a pseudonym, unless it was simply a mistake: they said he was called Abundance, perhaps thanks to some former neighbours in Mazan who, I found out later, were only too happy to open their doors to gossip-hungry reporters; they told them we had money, a swimming pool and a red convertible, and that I wore fancy clothes like a Parisienne.

The article, filled with information that had clearly been leaked, included extracts from the statement taken at my first interview at Carpentras police station. Reading between the lines it became clear that several photographs of the rapes had also been leaked. Over the course of a few paragraphs I became nothing more than the 'poor woman' or 'poor Marie', the victim I had never wanted to be, which of course I am, legally speaking, but not in the way I live my life. No matter. I turned the pages in one direction then another, and noted that my lawyer had been willing to respond to questions and had declared that I was only coping thanks to the love of my children. I recognised the cul-de-sac bordered with cypress and olive trees where we used to live, the Carpentras supermarket where we did our grocery shopping and where it had all started. But more importantly, I caught a glimpse for the first time of five of my rapists. One was grilling sausages on a barbecue. His face was blurred out, like Dominique's. They all were for me anyway: a crowd of faceless men whose names I could not yet recall.

About forty men had already been arrested. My lawyer kept sending me the transcripts of their interrogations; they read like strange truths, scenes with me but without me. I found out that one of the men had HIV. He had come to our house several times and never used a condom. By some miracle he hadn't infected me. I also realised that another man who had raped me used to greet me very politely at the boulangerie in Mazan; I recognised him because he once came to the house to buy some bicycle wheels. He'd come twice, in fact. I now know that the wheels were just an excuse, an idea of Dominique's: the guy wanted to have a look at me, to inspect the merchandise – there is no other way of putting it – before raping me. The worst thing, though, was that most of the men denied the charge of rape, and several claimed that I had been moving, participating in their orgy. My lawyer warned me it wouldn't be easy and that I would be under suspicion as well. I wasn't expecting that.

*

A HYMN TO LIFE

When the magazine came out, I took refuge in Caroline and Pierre's holiday home on the Ile de Ré, in the little town of Loix on the north of the island. I settled in at the end of summer, in September. It had been almost a year since my whole life had blown apart. I didn't want to be a burden to my children; each day I felt more urgently the need to be alone. So I suggested to Caroline and Pierre that I rent their little house, not knowing how long I would stay, and they agreed. For the first time in my life I found myself living alone. I wrote 'Guillou' on the letterbox. The summer season was over. The days were getting shorter. Calm was returning to this patch of land dotted with salt marshes like cloudy mirrors that turn pink every evening as the sun is setting. I was living on an island. I felt like a tiny island myself, or rather I wanted to be one, to be cut loose from the mainland, from other people, in other words from the rest of the world and all the human filth that had swamped us, my children and me.

Over there Dominique was in prison; over there the list of men who had abused me, some of them younger than my children, grew longer every week; over there the media were greedy for more and more details. After *Le Nouveau Détective*, the Vaucluse section of *La Provence* and *Le Dauphiné Libéré* seized upon 'the Mazan rapes'. Dominique was described as a retired electrician. He became 'the monster', 'the wolf of Mazan'. Every word written about him took on a particular meaning for me, the person who had shared his life for so long. He hadn't managed to escape any of it after all: the job as an electrician he had been so desperate to move on from, the father whose violence he now embodied and whose same terror he now inspired. Time was looping back on itself. Past and future met, engulfing everything we had strived for.

I wasn't sure this island could save me. It was contaminated. We had just found out that Dominique had once organised my rape in the very house where I was now seeking refuge. We had been looking after our grandson for the last week of the summer holidays before his parents came to pick him up for the beginning of the new school year. I remember the date because it was my name day, Sainte Gisèle, in 2018. Dominique and I stayed on for a few days after they left. A video shows a stranger raping me in my daughter and son-in-law's bedroom. I am wearing garters, torn stockings and black lingerie. Dominique must have brought the paraphernalia with him; he had not been seized by a sudden impulse, he had known all along that the nice grand-père he was for the first week was going to turn into the monster in the second. And that the monster was going to open the front door stark naked. It is described in the court transcripts. He was no longer abiding by any rules of common decency; he reigned over the night like an animal. He must have already raped me before the stranger arrived. He imposed his ritual on the man: he had to undress as soon as he entered the house and make a neat pile of his clothes to be sure that he didn't leave anything behind when he left. Afterwards the monster struggled to make way for the husband. Back home in Mazan, I couldn't remember if I had emptied the bins before we left, so I sent a note to Caroline and Pierre to apologise in case I'd forgotten. In fact I had emptied them, but under the influence of the pills Dominique had ground into powder and mixed into my last meal just before we left. I only came round five hundred miles later, at home in Mazan. There is a video taken during our journey: my unconscious body lies on the reclined front seat of the car. He is raping me in a car park.

I could not be an island.

When the examining magistrate, Gwenola Journot, summoned me back to Avignon a month later, in November, she asked me how I was dealing with all the media coverage. I told her about the strange sense I had that they weren't talking about me, but someone else entirely. It was not the same as the feeling of dissociation that my brain had granted me in Deputy Sergeant Perret's office in Carpentras; what I felt now was rage. For as the story spread, I was appalled to see that more and more people were saying that I could not have been completely passive. I was starting to appreciate the ordeal that women go through when they report an abuser – confronting a police officer or even a family member or friend with only their honesty, their courage and their bruised body and memory. In my misery, I had no need to say or prove anything; the police had done this already, they had damning evidence, appalling images that I was incapable of looking at, which they had gone through one by one to the point of making the investigators want to vomit. Later I heard how gruelling it had been for them to spend entire days extracting the photographs, videos and messages from Dominique's computer, phone, camera, memory cards and USB sticks, and then to look through it all, examine it second by second, month by month, year by year. They are trained to investigate crimes, not to witness them. And yet, despite everything, I would still have to convince people. The faint refrain of the accused kept rising, carried by their lawyers and – more wounding still – by what people so casually call 'common sense'. Again and again those anonymous voices returned to me, whispering that I could not possibly have forgotten. Impossible, they insisted. For many, the idea of a macabre procession of men approaching the bed of a lifeless woman was unbearable, inconceivable. She could not, in their eyes, be entirely innocent.

'What would you like to say to the men who question the claim that you were unaware of anything at all for the ten years during which the events took place?' the magistrate asked me.

'What do you want me to say to them? In the few photographs I've seen, I look dead, or as good as dead, at the very least in a coma.'

Who could I speak to about my shame? Sometimes I'd wake up in the morning and my pyjamas were soaked. I couldn't understand what was happening. It was as if I had wet myself in my sleep, as if I no longer controlled my ageing body. Not a single doctor had been able to allay my concerns.

The magistrate persevered. She told me there was one defendant who had sworn to her that he had seen me make an inviting gesture; he was even prepared to discuss this with me in a face-to-face confrontation. I replied that this was pure intimidation and asked whether such a hand movement was visible in the videos I didn't want to see. Obviously not.

The idea of watching them myself, as she kept suggesting, was still more than I could stomach. The detailed interviews with the criminals, relayed to me one by one as each man was arrested, and these discussions with the magistrate, were more than enough. Quite sufficient to haunt me. Afterwards I could only recall fragments, I couldn't take it all in, it was too crude, too violent, too many men, too many times. One part of me didn't want to get swept away, another part was only just waking up. That was when I remembered that a crown on one of my teeth had come dangerously loose during the months of lockdown when it was so hard to get an appointment with a dentist. Dominique had wrapped his fingers in a piece of gauze and gently prised it off. To think that I believed he was being kind and helpful! In fact the crown had come loose under the violence of penises being repeatedly forced into my slack mouth. And I finally worked out why I kept waking up soaking wet. Once they had finished their filthy business, and the other pervert had left, Dominique would take the lingerie off me, give me a vaginal douche with an enema bulb and put my pyjamas back on. There was no reason for me to be ashamed. My body was telling me what was happening but I couldn't understand its message. I didn't need the videos on top of everything else I was imagining. I didn't want to witness the evil things they had done to me.

The magistrate went on to tell me about some new photographs of Caroline and my daughters-in-law, Aurore and

Céline. She asked me if I wanted to see them. I said yes. With a tiny spy-camera pen placed in a toilet bag, he had taken pictures of them in the shower, both at our house and at theirs. With his mobile phone set up on the bedside table, he had filmed Caroline getting dressed in the guest bedroom in Mazan. He had gone further. He had photoshopped images of mother and daughter side by side, in lingerie, and posted the pictures on the internet. The magistrate read a message he had sent to one of his contacts: 'You like comparisons, here you go. I made this one of my bitch and her daughter, she had no idea I took the picture.' His daughter was just my daughter now, which was presumably what made it possible for him to serve her degrading, stolen image up to the sexual predators flocking to him on the dark web, and to claim to be a father the next morning. But I was still his bitch.

'What do you have to say to this?' the magistrate asked.

'What do you want me to say? It's so sordid, there isn't anything to say.'

There was nothing sacred left. He had sullied everything. All of us. Every room in the house. Our bedroom. The room his children slept in. The magistrate read me Dominique's statement after she had showed him those images. He told her he had shared them on the internet a few times, 'but not that many'. He acknowledged this was deviant behaviour. He insisted he had never drugged or touched his daughter.

'What do you have to say to this?' the magistrate repeated.

'I don't have an answer, about her, I don't have an answer.'

'Did you ever sense that your husband might be attracted to his daughter or daughters-in-law?'

'Never.'

I said he was a pathetic creep. The thought crossed my mind that he must have sat opposite her in the very room I was sitting in now. On this very chair, perhaps. Did he perch on the edge of the seat like you do when you're ill at ease, or did he lean against the back rest? Was he handcuffed? The magistrate told me Dominique had brought up doubts about Florian's paternity.

I was horrified. 'Next thing you know this will all be my fault! It's absurd. Nothing makes sense any more.'

'You pointed out that he didn't even spare you on special dates – it happened on your saint's day, Valentine's Day, your birthday. What do you have to say about that?'

'He had no boundaries any more. I don't know how far he would have gone if he hadn't been caught in the supermarket. I think I'd probably be dead by now.'

In conversation with her, it was all about my torturer and the pack of bastards that he communicated with on the dark web. It was almost simpler that way. When I talked to her, everything was simple, I felt nothing but disgust. I was even able to face up to the thought that he might have killed me. But I knew full well that as soon as I was alone I would go back to thinking about the man with two faces, the rapist and the man I used to call Doumé. I knew that the beaches of the Ile de Ré would always remind me of our long walks, playing board games, our fits of the giggles, Maxime asking for yet another ride on the merry-go-round. And afterwards, as it got dark, I would begin to wonder what would have happened had I suddenly woken up to find a stranger in my bed – whether Dominique would have killed me. What was he thinking about as he watched me as I lay unconscious after his crimes had been committed? I can't stop asking myself these questions, and more than anything, I can't stop wondering what I could have done, or said, or even simply what I might have seen.

There was the night when as we were having sex he whispered in my ear his fantasy of watching me being sodomised by a Black man. What if I had looked him in the eye then? I was shocked and hurt to know that while we were making love he was imagining me with someone else, imagining handing me over to another man who would do the thing I refused to have done to me. Our intimacy had no meaning any more. I didn't move. What would I have seen on his face if I had removed his hands from my body, turned on the bedside lamp, spun around and said, 'What on earth are you talking about?' Would I have seen the grotesque smirk of the rapist come into focus? Would I have been able to make the mask slip? I will never know. I let it go that night. The next day I decided not to talk about it; I thought about bringing it up but I didn't dare, I was still mortified. I was probably afraid of what it might reveal, or simply afraid of him. I let it go with a sense of bitterness against myself, and dumped it on to the garbage heap of male fantasy. Now I wonder if it hadn't already happened. I think it must have done; in fact, I have seen it in the photographs, so surely it had already begun by then. He was letting me know in a half-whisper, but there was no way I could understand. It was inconceivable.

'Did you ever notice a tendency on your husband's part to lie?' the magistrate asked.

'No. Half-truths, yes, but outright lying, no.'

Today, I don't think I would be able to make the distinction between a lie and a half-truth. But when I said that, I was alluding to moments during the last few years when I would come upon him sitting alone, sombre, lost in thought. If I asked him what was wrong, he would be evasive, say everything was fine, and that was enough for me. I always put it down to our financial worries. What I didn't tell the magistrate, though she must have suspected it, was that even since the revelation of all that had happened, I was still trying to detect doubt and regret in him; I wanted to believe that what I saw was him fighting his alter ego, swearing to himself that he would never hurt me again. Perhaps it was the opposite, a sign that the worst was yet to come, the prelude to the transformation, but I was desperate to believe the opposite. It was my way of shielding myself when I was alone.

I clung to the memories of our shared laughter, of moments of intimacy. It was him, it was me. Obviously there could be no ulterior motive, not that time. In November 2017, we were going home from Caroline's house on Ile de Ré, driving back to Mazan. It was All Saints' Day and I wanted to clean and put flowers on my mother and brother's grave, so we drove through the Indre and stopped at Azay-le-Ferron, where it had all begun. We felt like survivors, people from both here and there. Then we drove to Châtillon-sur-Indre to do the same thing for Dominique's parents' graves – really for his mother, in fact – but on the way, when we went to buy some chrysanthemums, our debit card was declined. We had reached our overdraft limit. So when we got to the cemetery, we borrowed the bouquet from the neighbouring tombstone, just for a moment, long enough to share some quiet thoughts, and to laugh. We laughed so much as we moved the flowers from one gravestone to the other, laughed as we thanked the gentleman next door, laughed at our bank for forbidding us this small gesture for his parents, laughed at them, and at ourselves as well, laughed nervously and painfully at the violence that haunted the past, and was buried at last. I thought we had learned how to live well, and evil was now rotting underground. And yet it was growing right there beside me. I now know that in 2017 the frequency of the rapes began to accelerate. By then Dominique had started to make contact with the worst kinds of men, feeding his most depraved fantasies, a far cry from the shy, gentle electrician I had met in the Indre.

After our visits to the cemeteries, we went into town to the nursing home to see my Aunt Jeanne, with whom I had stayed after my mother died, before my father took us to live in Paris. She didn't hear us come into her room. She was shrunken and emaciated, sitting with her back to us, looking out of the window. 'Jeanne?' I called out softly. 'Gigi!' she exclaimed as she turned around, and her voice held all the warmth and goodness that she had wrapped me in when I was nine. Then, looking up at Dominique, she asked, 'Who's that?' She didn't recognise him. At the time, I thought it was because his hair had gone white, or because she was so old. But now that I know what was going on in his head that year, how he had become my tormentor, I wonder whether my aunt, who had protected me during the worst time of my life, had had the clairvoyance of those who are about to leave this world. They see the true nature of things. If she hadn't recognised the man I had married, perhaps it was because he was not the man standing at my side that afternoon.

The interviews with the magistrate lasted three or four hours. We were beginning to get into the violence of the evidence. I would come out exhausted, usually around 6 p.m. Sometimes I stayed with my friends Brigitte and Guy near Avignon and only left the following day. Seeing friends made the ordeal easier to bear. One day, their son said to me, 'I am ashamed of being a man.' I told him he shouldn't be. That day I took the high-speed train to Paris and spent the night at Pascale's house. I left straight away the next morning. I had a meeting on the island with a therapist someone had recommended to me.

Still shaken by my conversation with the magistrate, I told her the whole story. I was immediately struck by the impression that she didn't believe me. She gave off a sense of authority, and I was convinced she thought I was a compulsive liar. 'Google Mazan, you'll see,' I said. At last I'd found a use for the publicity that so horrified me. She did a quick search and saw the headlines. Now I was an enigma to her. To her *as well*, I should say. She couldn't work out how I was still holding up, by what magic, or rather by what mechanism. I smiled as I explained that it was very difficult and painful, but everything would be all right in the end.

I said pretty much the same thing to Françoise, Pascale's sister, who lived year-round on the island and whom I saw frequently. To Geneviève too, Dominique's half-sister. We had taken to speaking on the phone once a week. I always felt as if we were talking about the same man – she knew better than anyone where Dominique came from; this whole affair was reawakening within her the shadows of her youth, the danger of Denis Pelicot, everything she had fled. Like me, she felt she needed to speak to her brother, she had so many questions. She told me she'd like to visit him in prison, but she was in hospital – she was over eighty and had a weak heart – so instead of visiting she wrote to him. The magistrate read me a passage from one of Geneviève's letters that she pulled out of a file – they had all been handed over to her, because correspondence sent to a prisoner is always opened before being delivered. This letter had been photocopied and added to the file. In September 2021 Geneviève wrote, 'Gisèle's doing well. You're lucky, she only wants to hold on to the good memories of you.' The magistrate was struck by this sentence and asked me to explain my sister-in-law's assessment of me, which she shared and which, I sensed, disturbed her. I said I didn't want to give the impression that I wasn't okay. I told her I was talking through my pain with my therapist. But even she found it hard to understand me. I left it to them to figure out my pride, my reticence, my lines of flight.

I walked. Even more than before. I love the island for its

long beaches, its changing skies, and the certainty it gives you that the clouds will not hover above your head for ever, that the weather will turn and chase them away. I walked for hours through the forest and across the dunes, to the sound of the surf and the tides. It is only by moving, by scouring myself with the elements, that I am able to confront my grief. When I am indoors, or with another person, I keep it at bay. As if the trap will snap shut again, as if the game was up long ago, the day I learned of my mother's death when I walked out of one room and into another. And that inconsolable little girl is still buried deep inside me, the child whom no one and nothing has been able to comfort ever since, not even love, not even friendship, not even motherhood.

The little nine-year-old girl is still here, restless within me. She has peopled my nightmares with armoured tanks and men who are hunting me down. She has kept me from sleeping since Papa's death. How hard I have tried to hush her voice and her pain. All my life I have warded off silence with music, fought insomnia with the hum of the radio, filled the empty spaces of daily life with cooking and tidying, chasing away dust, crumbs, mess, creases, weeds. I must seem obsessive, but keeping everything spick and span is vitally important to me. A single grain of sand could ruin everything and the little girl's fears would catch up with me again.

And now that everything has collapsed, that girl wants only to scream – or perhaps she wants to rejoice, since for ten years my sleep has been a kind of execution. There are only the two of us left. Only her and me.

So I would go out, and with a slow but steady step, leaving

no trace in the sand, I walked. I soothed her, rocked her, exhausted her, lulled her to sleep. I fought against her and for her. I asked compassion of no one. I kept going.

There aren't many people left on the island as the days begin to draw in. We see one another from a distance, find ourselves crossing paths at the same time every day by force of habit; our dogs sniff each other, we chat about them, their ages and breeds, then a little about ourselves. Eventually we exchange names, and wave in the direction of the house we live in. One day we go for coffee and begin to open up a little. 'Were you married?' 'Did you own your own home?' 'Did you have to sell in order to buy here?' Questions that reek of affluence, property deals, gilded retirement plans. But I had nothing now. I had never really owned anything anyway, and I was still dealing with my debt management plan, having lodged an appeal against the initial assessment of what I owed. So I remained evasive. I chattered away about other things. My story was making headlines, but it was simply impossible for me to talk about it.

I made new friends nevertheless. I accepted the odd invitation. I discovered that a small door can open on to a large courtyard and a vast house as beautiful as in any magazine. It was a different world, yet it adopted me. I let it happen. It was as if I had two parallel lives. And I pushed back against any questions as best I could.

With Angèle and Fred, who rented a little house up the road, I felt free to be a bit more open about myself, to display some vulnerability, I suppose because I knew something about theirs. They were the same age as my children but, with other lives and painful divorces behind them, like me they had come to the island to escape. They had slept in their car until they'd found a place they could afford. Angèle cleaned for a few families to make ends meet, and Fred harvested potatoes or worked in the vineyards depending on the season. One day I told them I'd been struck head-on by a high-speed train. It's an image I like to use to describe what happened. It's obvious that it means something serious, a real bloodbath, and there's no need to say anything else. Angèle took it almost literally, she thought I had been in a terrible accident. She didn't say anything but thought that the surgeon who had rebuilt my face had done an excellent job. And so my new friends came to understand that I would need a little time to explain my solitary presence on the island.

Winter was setting in. It would soon be too cold to get around on foot or by bicycle. I needed to start driving again, so I could go shopping, get to my therapist or the train station. I had hardly dared get behind the wheel after I'd lost control of my car between Carpentras and Mazan in the summer of 2018. Dominique had gone to buy groceries at that cursed Leclerc supermarket. He came home and told me he'd locked his keys in his car and someone had given him a lift back. I don't know how much of that to believe now, but in any case we had to go back with the spare key. We took my car, but he drove. On the way home, we agreed I would follow him. As I pulled out of the car park I hit a low wall. After that everything went from bad to worse. I couldn't steer straight, and he watched in his rear-view mirror as I drove dangerously close to the ditch, then veered into the opposite lane until I was hitting the plastic bollards that line the side of the road. Dominique switched on his hazard lights, got me to slow down, and we both stopped. I watched him run towards me with tears in his eyes. 'You're going to kill yourself!' Yes, I could have died, and it would have been because of him, although I didn't know it at the time, but it is clear now that I was under the influence of the drugs he was feeding me. Perhaps a rape had taken place the previous night, or there was one planned for that evening. It didn't stop him genuinely weeping at the thought that I might have driven into the ditch. And now I will live out the rest of my days with that double face: the one that wept, and the one that was slowly killing me.

I had no need to be afraid of driving now that my past blackouts had an explanation. And yet the sense of danger remained etched inside me. But I needed a car on the Ile de Ré, and ended up buying Caroline's little runaround. I made my way carefully along the island roads, glad when I found myself behind a tractor slowing down the traffic, then with increasing confidence. I was no longer scared of having an accident.

I decided to stay on the island for Christmas and New Year. I would greet 2022 facing the sea, the way one looks into the unknown. But Caroline wanted to use her house for a week during the holidays, and asked me to make myself scarce. I found myself with nowhere to go. I looked at hotels, mobile homes, campsites, but everything was either shut or already full. It was Angèle and Fred who offered me their house. They gave me the keys and their cat to look after while they were away.

It was then that I began to feel the strength of these new bonds. I realised that it is possible to spend Christmas far from one's family and still love them. That you can find comfort in sitting alone in the evening, nibbling on toast with cheese and a tomato, without having to look after anyone else. And most of all that I needed a place of my own.

'Tell me about your childhood,' my therapist said to me during our third session.

And that was how she began to understand the life force within me.

TWELVE

When the phone rang that October evening in 2022, I was curled up on the sofa with the flu. It had been a cold, damp autumn on the Ile de Ré. I didn't recognise the number, and I hesitated before answering. Eventually I picked up. A man's voice introduced himself as a police officer. It's about your husband. Yes, I said. It's always about my husband when the police call. No, this has nothing to do with the ongoing case, the policeman said. He told me he worked in Nanterre, in a unit investigating unsolved and serial crimes. Actually that was the first thing he said, so I should have known another storm was brewing; Nanterre was a long way from Avignon. I just hadn't taken it in. I was too under the weather to pay proper attention. But every word he was about to utter was going to tear my life apart again. He brought up some cold cases from years ago, an attempted rape, a murder. He mentioned the 1990s. He gave me the name of one of the victims. I couldn't grasp what he was saying, it had nothing to do with me. And then he said that Dominique was the principal suspect in both cases. It seemed utterly unreal, as if his words were being filtered through a feverish haze. I felt numb. I lay on the sofa, unable to move. At least I didn't have to worry about collapsing when the policeman told me that a few weeks earlier Dominique had confessed to the attempted rape.

I heard him say that he'd like me to come to Nanterre for questioning. I heard myself tell him that I lived a long way away and wasn't well enough to travel. He didn't insist. He said he would come to see me on the Ile de Ré. I hung up, my chest burning. When was this all going to stop? How many circles of hell were there in the pit I had fallen into two years ago?

The next morning, when my lawyer called to discuss the new development, I gave her short shrift. I was exhausted and unwell, and the one thing I wanted to avoid was her commandeering the situation. I didn't want to talk about it with her. I couldn't bear to listen to her laying it on thick, the way she did every time she read me yet another confession from one of the men who had raped me. This was a different case, nothing to do with her, though it clearly had something to do with me. But I needed room to breathe.

I had in fact been breathing more easily of late. I was no longer living in Caroline's house. A couple of months earlier, I'd moved into a little three-room house just around the corner that adjoined a larger house built around a courtyard. Unlike most of the people I knew on the island, Patrice and Eric, the owners, knew what had happened, and when they heard that I was looking for somewhere they suggested I move into this little house. They even decided to build a wall in the courtyard to give me more privacy, with a door at one end so I could easily be in contact with them and the rest of the property whenever I needed. I loved the little sunny courtyard where I had my coffee in the morning if the weather was fine. This house became my bubble, a breath of fresh air that had nothing to do with my previous life and offered me hope for the future. For the first time since I had fled Mazan, I felt at home.

In the meantime, my debt situation had improved slightly. I put together a management plan myself, as I couldn't afford a lawyer. Françoise gave me a lot of help with gathering supporting documents and evidence of debt. In my defence, I furnished the tribunal with the newspaper articles about the Mazan rape investigation. I hated them, couldn't bear what they brought to light, but I made use of them all the same. The tribunal hearing took place in March. There were so many other people there. So many debt-ridden people. I waited my turn, surrounded by those who had also come to plead their case: they couldn't pay their rent on time; there'd been a divorce, they'd lost their job, been on long-term sick leave, had an addiction. All those slippery slopes seemed quite benign compared to my situation, just the banal twists and turns of ordinary life. I'd never asked anyone for anything. I envied all those people their problems. I had never believed in unadulterated happiness. Both love and adversity had been my inheritance. When it was my turn to be heard, I asked permission to move closer to the judges' bench. I didn't want to explain what had happened to me in front of everyone else in the room, that my husband was in prison because for ten years he had drugged me, raped me and invited other men to rape me. The shame I felt was still overwhelming. I was allowed to move closer and explain my story in a whisper. Clearly, the judges had not gone through every applicant's file with a fine-toothed comb, and they hadn't noticed the newspaper articles I had slipped into mine. I saw the expressions on their faces change. I was told that Dominique had paid the outstanding balance of his tax bill since being in prison, and it now fell to me to repay 350 euros a month over a period of four years.

That was bearable, a much smaller sum than originally demanded. I'd been right to appeal. I was still hiding behind a pseudonym. At first I was the 'victim', or the 'spouse', then I became Marie P., chosen in haste six months earlier when the media first got hold of the story. Caroline took it up with me one day when I was visiting her in Paris. Marie was the name of her first cousin, Joël Pelicot's daughter. She was furious and concerned about her reputation. I made the mistake of responding that it was my middle name, and there was no risk of her cousin being mistaken for me, since she was much younger and had never lived anywhere near Mazan. Caroline flew off the handle and threw me out of her house. When Pascale came to pick me up, she found herself an impotent witness to the wretchedly complicated relationship between me and my daughter, whom she had known since she was a little girl. Each of us locked inside our own grief, as if we were being borne off on two opposing currents, with very different survival strategies. 'Pretend you're suffering, it'll do her good,' our lawyer suggested to me one day. But I was suffering! Keeping going, hanging on, putting on a brave face was all I knew how to do, and it was what I wished for my daughter too.

Eventually, after yet another argument, I stopped being Marie P. and decided to be known as Françoise P. It was my second middle name and that of the grandmother I had never known, my father's mother, who died when he was seven. I was no longer concealing my identity behind the grandmother who had lit up my childhood, but behind a ghost.

In any event, the media frenzy was at last beginning to abate. The spate of arrests had come to an end. Some fifty men were now behind bars; another thirty who can be seen in the videos proved impossible to identify. I couldn't stop thinking about those filthy bastards walking free. What further crimes were they committing, who were they going to rape? They must have been fully aware of the case. To know they were at liberty out there in the world triggered waves of panic. What if they tried to find me? What if they wanted to hurt me? I knew I was being irrational; they would be much better off keeping their heads down given the terrible things they had done to me. Then I would return to my daily life, the small things. Mornings, afternoons and evenings. On sleepless nights, when it's better to get up than to toss and turn, I would push open the courtyard door, go into Patrice and Eric's laundry room, plug in the iron to flatten everything, smooth everything, and cry in secret while waiting for the first rays of the morning sun to appear. My only compass was the slow drip of time passing, and at moments it even seemed to offer me a few promises – if only because I was still alive.

I still took long walks, alone or with my friend Françoise, Pascale's sister, and my panting bulldog. A white patch had appeared on his muzzle since he had lost his master. How could I explain to a dog what had happened? I didn't know, although I did sometimes find myself saying I'm dog-tired of the whole thing. I had no idea what Lancôme was feeling, but it seemed to me that the spreading white mark on his coat was an expression of his pain. I hoped that mine was less visible.

Two weeks after the phone call I was summoned to the police station in Saint-Martin-de-Ré to be questioned by two officers from Nanterre. I could sense their discomfort. Their dread of layering the unspeakable on to the despicable, the fear that it would finish me off. And just as I had noticed in the expressions of so many other people, I could see their surprise that I was still standing. I had got over the flu. I was feeling much better. I was rebuilding my defences and my resilience. I listened more carefully this time: in December 1991, a twenty-three-year-old estate agent called Sophie Narme was drugged with ether, raped, strangled and stabbed to death while she was showing a client around an apartment in the 19th arrondissement in Paris. Almost eight years later, in May 1999, a young woman whose identity is now protected was similarly ensnared while showing a man around an apartment. She managed to fight him off and lock herself in a wardrobe. The man left. She had recognised Dominique from photographs published in the run-up to the trial. Initially he denied the attempted rape, but he was caught out by a DNA test and eventually confessed. He continued, however, to maintain that he had nothing to do with the murder of Sophie Narme, and the police didn't have enough evidence to charge him. The DNA samples taken from the dead woman had been lost, but the police detectives were too struck by the similarities between the victims and the methods of the two attacks not to pursue their investigations.

I confirmed that on the two dates in question Monsieur Pelicot and I were living together in a town just outside Paris, and that at the beginning of the decade Dominique was working as an estate agent, but by 1999 had stopped. They showed me a photograph of the Cartier watch worn by Sophie Narme. I had never seen it. They asked if Dominique was a tidy person, how he put away his clothes. The question surprised me. They explained that the second young woman he had attacked described how, after he had tied up her hands, the rapist had got undressed and neatly folded and stacked his clothes before he threw himself on her. I told the police officers about the valet stand in our bedroom where Dominique used to hang his suit. That was all. I didn't know what I was doing there. I sat up very straight on my chair, but inside me everything was collapsing like one of those children's games where you carefully build something and then knock the whole thing down with one wave of the hand.

Françoise was being questioned in the room next door. She had only met Dominique a handful of times, and knew him far less well than her sister, Pascale, did; she really had nothing much to say, and she had even booked a hair appointment for straight afterwards, thinking she'd only be at the police station briefly. It never crossed her mind that the police would keep her for three hours, trying to pinpoint some detail that might emerge from a sentence and become a key piece in the puzzle. Françoise had nothing to tell them other than that she had met a nice guy who'd given her some helpful advice when she was looking to buy an apartment near Paris. As for me, I told them I'd never seen any sign of bruising or scratches on Dominique, or any rips or marks on his clothes. I was questioned for five hours. It was dark by the time I left. A friend from Loix came to pick me up so I didn't have to go back to the house alone.

After I got home I poured myself a glass of wine and called Françoise to ask how things had gone for her. Then I called Pascale. I needed to talk, to purge myself, to go back over everything in my own words. I wondered aloud why he had never said anything to me. I could only imagine that before he had acted on his impulses, he must have had urges he'd tried to restrain; I might have been able to help him myself, or at least encourage him to seek help elsewhere. 'Stop trying to save the whole world,' Pascale begged me. She tried to make me understand that this was no longer just about my husband, it was about a dangerous man. The crimes were no longer confined to our bedroom, our house. This was no longer the tragic love story of Gisèle and Dominique, though they certainly had once existed and I loved them still, with their youth, uncertainty and hope. I even protected them to the point of seeing in everything that had happened to me – in all the evil things he had done to me with other men – a form of ghastly possession, the decaying of our love. I was his drug, the only power he had over life. It sickened me, it could have killed me, but it was still fundamentally about him and me.

The new inquiry told quite a different story. This was a sexual predator who preyed upon young women. I sensed in

Pascale's voice that she was doing everything she could to help me keep my head above water, even though she herself was at a loss for words. This was a leap into another dimension, where humanity no longer existed and language failed. I could barely breathe. My chest was so tight it hurt. I felt dismembered. Sometimes I was a headless body, chasing the idea that I might have saved him from his demons, at others I was a stupid woman who'd allowed herself to be manipulated, and was now eaten up with shame.

I felt so alone that evening after I hung up the phone. There was no point trying to sleep. Even in those circumstances, there was no way I was ever going to take the sleeping pills that Dominique used to ply me with. Not that I had any in the house. I watched the hours tick by. What does an hour hold? Or a minute, or a lifetime for that matter? I didn't know any more. I was losing my grip on reality. Everything was slipping away. It felt as if the sun would never rise again. My life was one long, endless night.

I didn't phone my children for a few days. I thought about them, about the devastating impact these revelations would have on them, how hard it was going to be. They would also be summoned for questioning. David, once so close to his father, was going to see Dominique's face pinned up on the wall in the police station alongside photographs of other notorious serial killers and rapists. But I wouldn't be able to console him any more than he could console me. Like Caroline and me, we now barely spoke. He had aligned himself with his sister and all her anger and suspicions that were gradually turning into certainties. But without evidence, without a confession, I could not bring myself to say that the irreparable had taken place. Yes, I so hoped that it hadn't happened. For her sake, above all for her sake. Our infrequent telephone calls always ended badly.

Tragedy had struck not only our current lives, but our memories too. David and Caroline were grappling with theirs, trying and failing to locate a red flag that might have alerted them, but finding only fragments of a happy childhood. I brandished the memories awkwardly in front of them, which made me feel better, but must have only made it all the more painful for them. They probably felt betrayed and at the same time guilty for all the laughter and fun they had shared with their father, and tainted by being the children of a man guilty of such crimes. They wanted to erase it all. And that erasure included me as well.

The only one of my children I could talk to without either of us becoming upset was Florian. Sometimes when we spoke we didn't even talk about the case. I could just ask what was going on with his children, how they were doing at school, their holiday plans, his creative projects. It was what I needed. To carry on living.

That also meant living with the thought that one evening Dominique had come back to the house in Gournay-sur-Marne that we loved so much and sat down to dinner as if nothing had happened, hours after he had tried to rape a twenty-year-old woman. So young. Now she was in my head too. But always out of focus. The thing I could see in sharp detail was the man who had undressed her and tied her up, the man she had fought off, the man whose testicles she had grabbed so hard he let her go. The man with whom I had spent my life. That day, he had beaten her so he could rape her, and then he must have come back to our house. How had he not cracked? How had I not noticed anything? I didn't forget the other young woman either. She was dead. But Dominique denied he had killed her, and the Nanterre police admitted they had no proof that he had, though they were still searching. Which left me with a faint shred of hope to cling to. Dominique was a rapist, but not necessarily a murderer. And once more I cut him in two, as if I were amputating a limb after gangrene had set in. Saving something of him was saving something of us, saving our skin and anything else that could be salvaged from the ruins of our life.

But our lives no longer belonged to us alone. Perhaps two weeks after my meeting with the policemen from Nanterre in November 2022, I saw my lawyer discussing our story on a sensationalist cable TV show called *True Crime Tales*. Another lawyer came on after her and made the connection between these two cold cases and the Mazan rapes. It was all too much. The glare of publicity that I was trying so hard to avoid. Things being conflated. I was certainly not seeking to deny anything – I didn't want to disguise the facts – but I wanted to be accorded a little time, restraint and discretion. I was going at the pace of the justice system, not the media. The woman they were talking about on television, who 'had been raped two hundred times', everyone constantly banging on about the number as if it was a world record – two hundred times! – was obviously me, but I couldn't reduce myself to that. I felt betrayed by the way my lawyer portrayed me. I was fed up with her sound bites, her willingness to speak into any microphone held out to her, the great battle between women and men she claimed to be waging. And I was still terribly angry with her for leaving Caroline alone for hours with the file of images of all the violence done to me. I didn't feel she was protecting us at all. The next morning, I sent her a curt message informing her that she no longer represented me. It was over.

Some of my friends went into a panic and told me I couldn't do this alone, that I didn't know anyone else who could represent me. I replied that I would speak for myself, if need be. I had no backup plan. I didn't for a moment imagine the judicial maelstrom that I was about to be sucked into. But I trusted my instincts. I could sense what was good for me and what wasn't.

It was the friends I'd made on the island who picked up the pieces. Within a matter of days someone put me in touch with a man called Antoine Camus. He was a corporate lawyer, rape cases were not at all his area of expertise, but my friend said I could call him for advice; she'd told him about me, he'd be happy to talk and would point me in the right direction. So one day, towards noon, I dialled his number. He listened as I told him what had happened, how my life had imploded, all the questions I had, and about the videos I couldn't bear to watch. He barely interrupted me. He came across as tactful and reserved. I asked him if he thought it was essential that I be represented by a woman. The answer was clearly no, given that after an hour of discussion he offered to take on my case.

He explained that he would join forces with a colleague who was more experienced than he was in the criminal courts. So now I had a new lawyer. And soon I would have two. My second lawyer was also a man, called Stéphane Babonneau. A few days later, the three of us had a video call. They were in their office in Paris, and I was in my little house on the Ile de Ré. Two dark-haired men smiled at me from my phone screen, while being careful to maintain a tone of professional detachment. I was old enough to be their mother. Once again, I was frightened at the thought that they would watch the videos, ashamed that they should see me like that. But this time I felt a sense of reserve emanating from their side of the screen too. I had the unfamiliar sensation of taking charge, such a contrast to the last two years of doing whatever I was told. Finally things were starting to come together. But the past was getting even darker.

THIRTEEN

I had never told anyone about a recurring dream I used to have when we lived in Mazan. A man and a woman turn up at the front door. They ask whether my husband is home. 'It's about a complaint to do with a woman,' they say.

And then I'd wake up.

The nightmare would fade and I'd get out of bed. In the kitchen, the breakfast table had been set the night before. It was doing its job: the day was already on track to be a good one. Dominique would probably go off with some local friends on one of his bike rides up Mont Ventoux. We were retired now and no longer had to worry about his professional misadventures. When we moved to Mazan in 2013, we left all that behind us, though his debts still pursued us.

And yet, he would sometimes heave a deep sigh and say that life hadn't been fair to him, he hadn't been given a chance. I hardly paid any attention. Even when he wondered aloud why my pension was higher than his when he had always worked so hard, I didn't respond. To my mind, if anything we were rather lucky to be where we were, together, alive, looking out on that magnificent landscape.

By this time my ordeal had already begun, though I knew nothing of it. My only concern was about my unexplained blackouts and memory loss. And of course I didn't connect them to that new obsession he had developed since we moved to Mazan, of taking pictures of me when I came out of the bathroom in my bra and pants. I didn't like it, I always asked him to stop, and he would eventually put away his phone. But always with a sigh, saying that I ought to be happy because not a lot of men our age still lust after their wives. He was flattering me and my fixation on happiness. As for the nightmares, I had always had them.

But that one came true. Ten years later, the police did call on me about my husband. They might have turned up twenty years earlier, if the investigation after Dominique had assaulted the young woman had come to anything. Time was nothing but a tangled skein.

I often think back to two occasions when Dominique came home crying. I'm pretty sure both times were during the 1990s, but I can't recall the precise dates. No matter how hard I try, or how often, I can't remember what year it was. Had he just committed the unthinkable? Had I completely missed something? Both times he told me he had lost his job and I did my best to cheer him up. I remember I was in the middle of making dinner. For me, the memory of Dominique's tears came to be associated with the delicious smell of gratin dauphinois baking in the oven, his sadness confused with the taste of comfort food, as if things could only get better. All's well that ends well around the dinner table.

I couldn't bear to see him so miserable. I needed to give him confidence, protect him. I suppose right from the start I was protecting him, when I'd send parcels from Paris containing a fancy cigarette lighter and a bottle of Fabergé Brut cologne to the young man adrift in the countryside. In a way he was always that young man in my eyes, and never more so than when he came home depressed after yet another setback. He aspired to much more than just another new job, I knew that better than anyone. He wanted to be an entirely different person, not an electrician who people called when something broke, like his father, the man who ended his working life fixing washing machines. But all his big plans came to nothing. I, on the other hand, worked hard and was steadily moving up the company ladder. I'd changed, I was stronger, I had new skills and more status. Dominique never openly expressed any bitterness or rivalry, but the further back I go, the more I can see how the arcs of our lives were diverging. And I see how I was trying to redress the imbalance between us. Trying to make him feel better about himself, time and time again.

At the end of 1999, EDF encouraged me to apply for a job in a newly created department for the supply chain management of components for nuclear power stations. I was told the job was mine if I wanted it, though I still had to go through the formalities of the application and interview process. I wasn't sure I did want it. I made up all sorts of reasons why I shouldn't apply. I didn't feel up to it. I wasn't ready for a promotion. It seemed natural to everybody else at work, but to me it felt like a leap into the void. It's not for me, I kept telling myself, erasing all thought of how far I had come, all the knowledge and skills I had acquired over the past twenty years. I shrank from the title of the new role they wanted me to take on: 'logistics executive'. It was so far from the lowly secretary I was when I first started, the diffident young wife working to top up her husband's salary. It was blindingly obvious how much I had changed, but I somehow found it difficult to come to terms with the woman I was now.

I was under pressure from within the company to go up for the job. Eventually I had the interview. It lasted for two long hours. When asked if I could see myself in this new position, I replied that I could, but I was sure I wasn't the most qualified applicant – there must have been others better suited to the role. I was still holding back, standing in my own way. But in the end I was the one they offered the job to.

'Why me?' I wanted to know.

'You were the most honest,' said Séverine Brachet. She was a young engineer who had recently graduated from a prestigious university, and we would be working together as a team from now on. I never felt any disparity between us, despite all her impressive degrees. We complemented each other: she was hot-blooded and liked to push things through by force of personality, while I, as always, smoothed things over. Everything pointed to the fact that I was right where I belonged working with Séverine. I had no reason to lack confidence at work. My insecurity came from elsewhere. Only I was bathed in the glow of success, while Dominique was still searching so desperately for it.

It was not long after I had started in my new role that Pascale came into my office to tell me I should be asking questions about my husband rather than always putting him on a pedestal. I think it was that word, pedestal, that I couldn't bear. No one had the right to insinuate that I had somehow misjudged him, to cast doubts on him or on our relationship, which was the foundation of my life. I was doing all I could to keep it strong. I would always protect Dominique from any criticism. Was it because the structure had already begun to teeter that I threw Pascale out of my office in such a rage? Did it take just one word from her to make it topple? I didn't want to hear anything about it.

Even if I had asked her a few questions that day, even if she'd told me that my husband had made advances towards her, it wouldn't have changed anything. I'd have told Dominique, he'd have lied, and we would have stayed together because that was what I really wanted, what I clung to. Maybe I would have kept Pascale as a friend. She probably wouldn't have come on holiday with us any more, or even been welcome at our house, and we would have needed time to adapt before starting again on a new footing, but our friendship wouldn't have been severed so abruptly. We would have seen each other at work, exchanged niceties, occasional bits of news, and gradually, without even noticing, we would have started confiding in each other again; maybe even more than before, as women do when they're among themselves, away from men, all the banal little everyday things that in my case, over time, might perhaps have alerted her.

Instead I chose to erase Pascale from my life. I told her never to speak to me again. I underestimated the importance of friendship. I don't think I was very different from many other women of my generation in this regard. The principal axis of our lives was the man we had married or were hoping to meet. And I went much further than that, locking myself into a long tête-à-tête with Dominique. Back then it was impossible for me to imagine that those who suffer could turn against the people who love them.

I drove home from the office that evening in tears. I asked Dominique to explain what Pascale might have meant. I wanted the three of us to talk things through. I thought he must have another mistress, which would have been the most straightforward and least upsetting scenario. I thought he was the one drifting away from me, rather than me from him. I couldn't forgive myself for the lover who had come into my life, and now I was rejecting the friend I'd thought of as a sister. Dominique didn't want to talk about it, he was furious with Pascale, said terrible things about her. It was all out of proportion, and so I chose to backtrack, to make light of it, as always. To preserve our relationship. I dropped the subject. And so Dominique drew me back to him, while I isolated myself from everyone else, without him even having to ask. As if we were just starting out in life, united against the whole world, each the other's redemption.

I had leapt for joy in 2003 when a man he'd met while he was working for the telephone company offered Dominique a job running his business. Dominique thought he was being handed an enormous amount of responsibility. But once again it didn't take long for it all to fall apart. He soon realised he was just a front man for the company. The person he had gone into partnership with was writing cheques left, right and centre. The business was foundering, and Dominique along with it. Months of unemployment followed.

By now our nest was almost empty. Caroline had recently met Pierre and moved in with him. David, who had moved out a long time before, was married to Céline. Florian was seventeen and still living with us, though in the way of teenagers he was hardly ever around.

Around this time, EDF announced that it was selling off its company housing. We urgently had to find a new place to live. By a stroke of luck, Céline and David, who both worked in property, soon found us a little house nearby in Noisy-le-Grand. We were able to carry on living close to the river Marne that we loved so much. Dominique was now spending all day on his own in the new house, which was empty of both children and memories.

The following year he was rushed to hospital with appendicitis. The surgeon called me immediately after the operation to tell me he had found a tumour and removed an entire chain of lymph nodes. Dominique had lymphoma. I decided not to tell him when he came round from the anaesthetic, and asked the doctor and our children to do the same, to give him time to regain his strength. I was afraid he would give up. When he was finally told about his condition he was surprised. 'You were full of smiles when you came to visit,' he said. My old defences in the face of illness, no doubt. My need to protect him, still.

He recovered well, and a year later decided to set up his own telephone and electricity company. It was a sign he was in remission. He suggested I take on the role of company director in name only, a proxy appointment he needed to register the company. But it was illegal for someone in full-time employment to do this, so he asked Florian, who was still a student. He agreed. The children were worried about their father and promised to help out. We were all in this together. The company was domiciled at our address. We had to move again, this time to another, larger house in Noisy-le-Grand that sat on a corner, meaning it had two front doors and two addresses, ours and that of the company. As if, at home, he had already taken on a double identity.

But it was for a good cause. He found a new business partner, rather more trustworthy than the last, who had links to an architectural firm that sent them clients. He even took on two trainees. The office was always busy. And the house filled up too, when Céline and David moved in with us while their new house was being finished. Céline was pregnant. Nathan was born on July 12th 2006. We were grandparents, we had a grandson, and I was overwhelmed with happiness. Once again we had a tiny little boy under our roof learning to smile. Everything was going well. Even Dominique's business was doing just about all right.

I laughed one day when he said to me, 'Why are you always in trousers? You really don't make the most of yourself. You ought to show off your legs.' I laughed but he was incredibly insistent. I told him to get lost when he suggested filming us having sex. But it didn't raise any suspicions. There was nothing unusual in couples wanting to spice up their sex lives. I sometimes overheard young women at work talking about these things, how they'd watch the video afterwards with their partner. I enjoyed spending time with women a decade or so younger than me, I liked their optimism and energy. Sometimes, listening to them, I found them more liberated, and I wondered if I was too prudish and inhibited. Dominique's suggestions occupied that grey area where the other person seems to be telling you how much freer and less uptight they are than you. But ultimately I had no problem refusing.

I thought things were okay between us, and we had got over the worst – infidelities, unemployment, bankruptcy, illness. We were still formally divorced and had never seriously considered getting married again until one day Joël's son, Adrien, Dominique's nephew, brought up the idea. He was very insistent about it, playing around with my lucky number seven, and eventually he came up with the idea of us holding the new ceremony on July 7th 2007. We did exactly as he suggested. Various people, particularly our children, had been asking for a while if we were going to remarry. It's difficult to imagine today but to lots of our friends we seemed like the perfect couple. They saw us laughing together, dancing *le rock'n'roll* or the Madison at the drop of a hat, whereas lots of people our age who had been together for as long as we had gave the impression they could barely stand the sight of each other. Caroline liked to tease us that we were still a couple of teenagers. I liked hearing her say that. Children have no idea what their parents were like before they came along, but we gave ours a glimpse of how genuine and strong our relationship had been from the moment we'd met.

Joël officiated in the ceremony room of his town hall in Charentilly, a little town in Indre-et-Loire that had been built around a chateau with round towers and pointy roofs and a large park, very similar to Azay-le-Ferron. The backdrop was the same, but time had passed. Joël's mayoral sash was a stark reminder that he was now a local dignitary, something that Dominique would never be – just one more thing to add to all the others that had marked their differences since childhood.

I'll never forget the day that Dominique accompanied Joël, then a newly qualified doctor, on call. Joël's car wouldn't start so he asked his father if he could borrow his, but Denis refused, and it was Dominique who offered to take him on his rounds in his 2CV. He drove his brother to wherever he was needed by his patients. For a few brief hours, he was in Joël's world. But only for a few hours.

By the time of our remarriage both men had grown portly and grey, but while Joël had been a doctor and a local councillor, not to mention the mayor for the last eighteen years, Dominique could still only fantasise about professional success. I lived with the ups and downs of his hopes and failures. On our second wedding day, under his brother's authority, he was symbolically formalising his sole accomplishment, which had reconciled him to himself and to life and distanced him from his childhood. In other words, us.

We celebrated our nuptials in a beautifully restored old farmhouse near Tours. It was a lovely party, a reparation in a way: the wedding we never had, the one that my father-in-law had denied us thirty-four years before. Now he had been dead for three years and couldn't hurt us any more. We didn't miss him. I did, though, miss my own father. Not a day goes by when I don't think of him, even today. Years afterwards, I had told him how Dominique's father had stolen our savings, and how sad I'd been at my own wedding; how I would have loved to have had long tables covered in white linen as he had requested, but that I'd decided not to say anything. 'If I'd known that,' he responded softly, 'I would never have given the marriage my blessing.' But I wouldn't have listened to him anyway. I wouldn't have listened to anyone. That was my whole story. And here I was, marrying the same man for a second time. We did not sing Michel Fugain's 'Une belle histoire', but an even older song, Edith Piaf's 'Mon Dieu', a plea to be allowed to see her lover again for just one day.

Within a couple of years, Dominique was no longer able to keep paying his trainees. When his business partner retired his clients vanished. He couldn't manage on his own. He asked me to help him out, so I took out a loan of 4,000 euros. Soon he was no longer allowed a chequebook. All the warning lights were flashing. I knew the story so well. Mainly I was worried for Florian, who was officially the company director. I didn't want him to start out in life burdened by his father's debts and failures. I raised the limit on my line of credit from the Sofinco consumer finance company, which meant we had access to a large sum of money, at eighteen per cent interest. The following year Dominique closed the office. Shuttered the company. He threw in the towel and took early retirement. Which meant that repaying his debts now fell entirely to me.

The rent was too high for us to carry on living in our house in Noisy-le-Grand. Céline found us a modest apartment in Villiers-sur-Marne. It was too small for Florian to live with us, but he was twenty-four and old enough to leave home – not that he was given any choice in the matter, or the freedom to make the decision himself. He moved in with his girlfriend, Aurore, not far from us. I had the sense that he was distancing himself from his father. He seemed resentful, though I couldn't put my finger on why. Sometimes he said, 'I did everything you expected of me,' and it was true. He had taken on considerable risk by becoming his father's front man. He began to realise this when the bank started to look more closely at the company's accounts. But now I know there was much more to it than that. Florian had seen the kinds of Google searches Dominique was doing online. Because he was in charge of fixing his father's computer when anything went wrong – he was the only one who knew what to do – he had discovered the keywords Dominique was using when he was looking for sex. This was in addition to the time when Aurore, Florian's partner, had walked in on Dominique masturbating. After that Florian stopped sniggering with the rest of us at Dominique's email address – 'Fétiche45' – which I was always nagging him to change. His father was diving deep into pornography as well as ruining us financially. But Florian hadn't dared to tell me about it.

I now know that Dominique was caught upskirting in a supermarket not far from our apartment as early as 2010, the year he stopped working, and that the security guards had called the police. I only found out about this in 2023, thanks to the investigation. Much too late.

A HYMN TO LIFE

If I had known at the time, my life would certainly have changed. I would have looked at him differently. I'd have pushed him to see a psychologist. I'd have questioned him about his relationships with women, and with me. But even then I would no doubt have been inclined to forgive him, just as I was ten years later, the afternoon I got off the train from Paris and he confessed what he'd been caught doing in the Leclerc supermarket in Carpentras. But at least the alarm bells would have begun to ring.

In 2010 the police clearly didn't think filming under women's skirts was terribly serious, because he got away with a fine of 100 euros, and I never heard a thing about it. I'd go into work early in the morning, leaving him on his own at home. He had retired but I was planning to carry on working for another two or three years. I didn't follow Séverine Brachet into new projects as she suggested because that would have meant too much travelling. I didn't want that: my priority was always our marriage and our home life.

It was when I began training the people who would succeed me at EDF that I realised how far I had come. Meanwhile Dominique and I were starting to think about where we were going to retire, mapping out the path that would lead us to Mazan.

We weren't old, not yet sixty, but we had reached the stage in life where everything finally seems to be falling into place. But there are things one forgets, things one wants to forget, dreams that tell us something about our vague, drifting anxieties that we don't pay attention to because we already have what matters most to us, a life that feels as if it was meant to be. If I had been asked to describe us then, I would simply have said we were an inseparable couple with three children and many grandchildren, the family of my dreams.

In 2011, when Nathan was five, Charlize and Clémence were born. There were no places at the crèche, so David and Céline asked us if we would take care of them during the week. Because Dominique wasn't working he looked after the twins by himself on Tuesdays, Wednesdays and Thursdays, from morning to late afternoon. We laughed whenever we saw that he'd buttoned up their dresses back to front. I loved that he was with his granddaughters, and looked forward to Fridays, when it was my turn. I was so happy to be basking again in the affection of little ones. Little did I know that my husband had already begun to drug me and film himself raping me. That he would even do so years later when the children were spending part of their school holidays in Mazan. He admitted it in court: he hadn't invited anyone over that evening; he had drugged and raped me while Nathan, Charlize and Clémence were sleeping in the next room. They came into my bedroom to wake me up the next day. Their grandfather had asked them to let me 'sleep', but they were surprised to find Maminou still in bed at noon. They slapped my cheeks, trying to get me to open my eyes, but in vain.

Is the shadow cast over my life nothing but an endless return to that moment, when the child tries to wake her mother – then her grandmother – from a suspicious sleep resembling death?

FOURTEEN

'How are you feeling about the trial?' Gwenola Journot, the examining magistrate, asked me.

'To be honest, extremely apprehensive. I don't know how I'm going to react. I have no memories of anything, but it will all become much more real when I see them standing there in court.'

'Are you ready to watch the video evidence of what they did to you?'

'No. I don't want to be traumatised for the rest of my life. In a way, watching them would be like being raped all over again. If they're shown during the trial I shall leave the courtroom. I do not want to see them.'

It was January 3rd 2023. According to the transcript, the interview was almost over. Stéphane Babonneau, my new lawyer, sat beside me. I told Journot that when the time came, I wanted the trial to be held behind closed doors. 'For the sake of my mental health, obviously, I won't be making any comments or having any contact with the media. I'll let my lawyers speak for me. I intend to be as inconspicuous as possible.'

It feels very strange to read those words today. It's me, I recognise myself. At that point I still believed that suffering must not show; it should stay hidden, like our grief at the loss of those we have loved. It hardens inside you and in turn hardens you. I had always lived like that, and I fully intended to continue doing so. I didn't yet realise that this time I wasn't confronting death, but a terrible poison. Unlike grief, it destroys your memories – all of them – one by one, until even your sense of self is gone.

The magistrate asked me if Dominique had ever told me that when he was thirteen and working on a building site he had witnessed the gang rape of a young woman. He had told her about it: how he had been made to participate, how the men had forced his face into the victim's vulva. It was like discovering the outcome of a story whose ending I had never heard before. Dominique had often brought up a peculiar memory of a building site where his half-brother, André, a carpenter, had helped him get a job. He was just a kid, and some of the guys had put him through a sort of initiation ritual. He never told me exactly what it was, he simply said he was frightened; he'd raised the hammer he happened to be holding and threatened to hit the first man to come near. He never went beyond that point in the story. He looked so sad whenever he talked about it. I sensed there was more to it than that, but I never pushed him to disclose anything further, and so I had never heard about any gang rape. But it didn't seem out of place in the picture I had of his youth. He was running away from something when I met him. And I wasn't surprised that he was now drawing on his childhood traumas to mount his defence.

I know the magistrate struggled to grasp how my mind worked. 'She thinks you're protecting your husband,'

Stéphane told me afterwards. I wasn't, of course. But it was so painful to listen to this, to know how he'd been subjected to male brutality. I had been his ally, his love, his passport to freedom, and now I was confronted with his crimes. I was simply trying to understand.

The magistrate had already moved on. It was the perpetrator she was interested in. I was hit with an avalanche of horrifying information. Dominique, in an act of sordid reciprocity, had raped the drugged wife of one of the rapists. He had forcefully instructed the men who raped me not to wear a condom. Some of the rapists had even stalked me: they wanted to see me in daylight, so Dominique told them when and where we did our shopping and they'd follow me around the supermarket. It was staggering to hear how his monstrous behaviour had consumed everything, invaded even the most basic aspects of our life. The magistrate showed me some photographs and asked if any of the faces were familiar. Of course they weren't. I'd never had any suspicions as I walked up and down the supermarket aisles, keeping a careful eye on our budget, completely oblivious to the people brushing past me. Their names meant nothing to me either. All those faces of all those ordinary men repulsed me. I didn't want to know anything about them. I wasn't ready for that. But I also knew that the moment I would have to face them in court was drawing near.

The magistrate told me that one of the men was insisting that I had consented. He claimed it was impossible for me to have been raped so many times over so many years without knowing what was going on, to be completely unaware that so many men were abusing me over such a long period of time. He said he had discussed it with other women, and they had all agreed it was impossible.

'What do you make of that?' she asked.

I don't know why she asked me what I thought. Perhaps it was to prepare me for their line of defence. I had no reaction except disgust. I said that the man who talked like that was a thoroughly vile person, and I was ready for a face-to-face confrontation if that was what he wanted. The saddest thing was that this view was being widely put about, which I knew because people saw fit to tell me. He must have known this too, and no doubt it emboldened him to reject the evidence of the images and arrogantly use women's words to back him up.

This was what awaited me.

I sighed deeply. 'I'll have to go through this with every single one of them at the trial, won't I? It's going to be unbearable.'

I often thought about what the forensic pathologist who had examined me early on had said. 'You know, whenever my husband brings me a croissant from the boulangerie in the morning, I always wonder what he's trying to hide,' she said. I'm sure she was married to a wonderful man, but by extending the suspicion to her own life, she seemed to be trying to protect me, to reassure me that as women we are all capable of being deceived. She had sensed, that day, that beyond the pain of the revelations and the shame of my body being turned into a sack, there was also the shame of having understood nothing – of feeling like an idiot in the eyes of others, and in my own. Professional experience had taught her about the loneliness that lay ahead for me, and the isolation that rape victims suffer.

How was I to stop the lie spreading that I had been aware of what was happening? How to describe my fear of dying, the twelve kilos I'd lost, the multiple gynaecologists and neurologists I had consulted, the inconclusive brain scan? How to explain that I had no idea that someone could love another and yet cause them so much pain? How, simply, to explain who I was? For fifty years, I had tried to find myself in a man's eyes. And he in mine – until he tried to extinguish them.

I wasn't afraid of Dominique. Of course, he was the leader of that disgusting pack of rapists – that I didn't deny – but because I knew him, I set him apart from the rest. I was eager to confront him. I had so many questions, for the sake of our shared history, our children, our marriage, even more so now that the Nanterre criminal-investigation unit was pursuing its own inquiries. Over the following weeks, the police interviewed my old friend, Pascale, and Dominique's half-sister, Geneviève. They both called to tell me. I know they also questioned Michèle, the woman he'd lived with for a few months after we had briefly separated. They were searching. Scouring every corner of his life. They wanted to charge him with murder.

A few months later, during the Easter holidays, two police officers turned up at Florian's house in Thenon, in the Dordogne. I was spending a few days there with the children. They needed to question us again. They showed us a photograph of a man we had sold a car to back when we were still living in Gournay-sur-Marne. It turned out that a few years later he had ended up in prison. We knew nothing about him. When they left they took with them Dominique's toolbox, which Florian had brought from the house in Mazan, but they found no clues there.

Through his lawyer, Dominique had requested the exhumation of Sophie Narme's body, so that a DNA test could be carried out. I chose to see this as a sign that he had nothing to hide. I needed to believe it. Even as I write this, I can hear the disapproval of people who think I am making excuses for him. I needed to tell myself that I had not spent my life with a murderer, and I was going to cling to that thought until it was proved otherwise. If the DNA test said it was Pelicot, if he ended up confessing, then it was Pelicot. I would not contest the facts, but first I needed them to be established.

It's me I am protecting. The few illusions I still have, however tenuous they may be.

Once I had returned to the Ile de Ré – once the magistrate and police officers were no longer summoning me for questioning, once I had gone back to living alone, once I'd forced myself to shake off my sorrow – I sometimes found myself making my way to the village of Saint-Clément, where there was a huge circus tent called La Java des Baleines. When night falls and the lights go on, it has all the majesty of an old-fashioned big top surrounded by the ocean. It's a good place to go for a drink or dinner and to listen to live music or see a show. I often went there with Françoise, Patrice, Eric and plenty of others, and sang and danced – not so much to forget, nor to bury the woman whom the expert psychologists had decided was submissive, whom the rapists called a liar, and whom the magistrate was struggling to understand, but because I have always loved to sing and dance, and I needed to do that now more than ever.

One evening in June, I found myself sitting next to a man I didn't know. His name was Jean-Loup. He was cheerful, good-humoured and discreet. He told me he didn't go out much, which explained why I had never seen him before, despite the many friends we had in common. It was a set-up, the kind of encounter arranged by people who mean well, but that almost always comes to nothing. This time, however, the plan was working perfectly. I imagined our friends exchanging gleeful, conspiratorial glances as we chatted. Our conversation flowed, subtly separating us from others at the table. There was only the very occasional moment of silence.

I asked all the questions. The first thing everyone always wants to know is how you ended up on the Ile de Ré. Jean-Loup told me he and his wife, Bénédicte, had spent many happy summers on the island with their two children, and eventually decided to retire there. They had sold their house near Versailles and bought a large property that needed a lot of work, but just as the renovations were coming to an end, Bénédicte's health suddenly deteriorated and she was diagnosed with an incurable and rapidly progressing degenerative condition. Jean-Loup soon found himself having to remind her of his name, and it was clear that they were not going to have the time together they had looked forward to. He fed her, bathed her and tended to all her needs until he was so exhausted that his own health began to suffer. He only agreed to put her into a nursing home after his children encouraged him to do so out of concern for his well-being. She died there, six months before I met him.

Jean-Loup didn't ask me any questions. 'I found out what happened to you from the papers,' he told me. Patrice and Eric had shown him an article from *Le Monde* before we met. They wanted to save me the ordeal of having to tell him what had happened. I felt so embarrassed that he knew, I worried that he would imagine things and see me as nothing but a victim, a defiled woman. But my fears soon evaporated – he didn't ask me anything about it and I didn't feel the slightest bit awkward. We had plenty of other things to talk about, most of them perfectly mundane. In fact, that was what made our conversation so enjoyable for the two wounded souls that we were. Later that evening La Java des Baleines became a disco. Every so often the lyrics of some old song popped into my head. We wandered up to the bar to order another crêpe. I never wanted this conversation to end.

Patrice and Eric had organised it all beautifully. Not long afterwards, the four of us went to see *Carmen* in Saint-Martin-de-Ré. We had dinner together, then Jean-Loup drove me home. He kissed me on the lips as we said goodbye. I was light-headed with happiness. I needed to love again. I wasn't afraid. I know only too well that my experience is proof that there are potentially violent rapists among us wherever we are. I know my story has fuelled disgust for men, but it has not done that for me. I know that the image the world had of me at that point was nothing more than of a woman who had been horrifically abused; if I had any memories of the ordeal, I'm sure that is what I would have been reduced to, and it probably would have killed me. But I was forged in a different time and place. The way I think about life was wrought at the moment of my mother's final breath, when Papa leaned over her and whispered her name, and I squeezed her shoulder and begged her to wake up. In that instant I felt a wave of infinite love wash over me, far stronger than death. That sensation saved me, carried me through, and no doubt also blinded me and warped my judgement, considering everything I endured with Dominique. And yet the feeling persists: love is not dead. I am not dead. I still have faith in people. Once, that was my greatest weakness. Now it is my strength. My revenge.

That summer we began a relationship. There was something hesitant about it, something gloriously tentative, as there often is when you meet someone new, but there was more to it than that. I was afraid of how Jean-Loup would feel about having a new woman in his life. He was worried about what being with a new man might mean for me. We went out to dinner, to the cinema, held hands, kissed, but we didn't take the plunge. We were too damaged. And then one day I said to him, 'Do you know what I want? To spend the night in your arms.'

He came over to my house. We didn't even eat. We couldn't wait. We were afraid too, of course. What remained on my skin of all that had been inflicted on me? Where was its trace, since it was not in my memory? Would Jean-Loup see it? Think about it? I sensed caution in him too. But my body yearned for the warmth of his embrace, transported me to some other place, did not remember. All the images, all the abuse, all the numbers that were now public knowledge, they had no place in my bedroom.

That first night was gentle, punctuated by stifled giggles and a few furtive tears. I was seventy years old and had slept with no one but my husband and my erstwhile lover. Jean-Loup was the third man in my life.

We waited a while before I stayed over at his house, where he had planned to live with his wife in their old age. There was a photograph of her in the living room. I didn't want him to take it down. I liked listening to him talk about her. I felt real affection for this man, who had taken such good care of his wife until she was so cruelly taken from him. He seemed to have emerged from a place far from this island where we had met: from a formative scene of my childhood, the source of my deepest pain. That is how I fell in love with Jean-Loup.

But soon afterwards he began having panic attacks and developing allergies. 'I feel like I'm cheating on Bénédicte,' he said. I suggested we take a break from seeing each other. I know how hard it is to let go of the dead. 'No,' he responded instantly. 'You mean so much to me.'

We talked a lot, but actually saying the words 'I love you' was very difficult. By some quirk of fate, he also had a little bulldog. Together we went for long walks. His dog was younger and a bit madcap; mine was slower and better behaved. I enjoyed hearing him reminisce. As a steward and then a purser for Air France he had been all over the world. He'd even flown on Concorde. His tales broadened my horizons. His children had followed similar paths: his son,

Victor, was a pilot, his daughter, Mathilde, a flight attendant. They came to visit when they weren't flying. During those times, I always made myself scarce. He didn't need to ask. I was only too aware of how my presence might upset them, when they were still seeking echoes of their mother in their father's company. Jean-Loup would call me the minute they left. There was something amusing, even a bit thrilling, in the way we kept our relationship secret, as if we were teenagers and our lives were just beginning. It couldn't last, but those feelings brought us closer. All over the island hollyhocks were growing up through the earth and the cracks in the pavements, reaching towards the sky with the same thirst for life as us.

That summer David and Céline decided to come and spend a couple of weeks on the island with their children. I was delighted. I missed them all so much. I couldn't put them up in my little house, but I found them a caravan in a beautiful campsite nearby. I hoped that their holiday would help us rediscover the joy of being together, despite all the pain. And that is what happened.

One evening I mentioned Jean-Loup. My son was ecstatic. He called his sister, who was just around the corner in her house. 'Come and see Maman, she's got something to tell you.' Over she came. I don't think she was expecting the announcement. 'I've met someone,' I said. She was overjoyed as well, and wanted to be introduced to him immediately. I was so relieved. Jean-Loup didn't live far away – not that anyone is ever far away on the island. He came straight over, and she asked him a barrage of questions. It felt as if everything was suddenly resolved; Jean-Loup was the saviour, filling the empty space at their mother's side, the abyss into which their father had dragged us all.

I savoured every moment of that summer. But when, in November 2023, I saw photographs of my and Dominique's second wedding in *Paris Match*, I understood that the demolition process wasn't over yet. There I was, my face blurred out, on the arm of Dominique – whose face was not – wearing the elegant flowery dress that had been specially made for me by a local seamstress. Forced into the limelight, plastered over every newspaper kiosk in France.

I knew who had given the pictures to the magazine. It was Joël, who had married us that day. He was interviewed in the article, calling himself Thierry. I was still Françoise. Only Dominique was Dominique P. His elder brother recounted their happy childhood, describing how they roamed freely in the great outdoors, built huts and fished for frogs. 'I've tried to work out what the trigger was that might explain everything, but I can't. Nothing strikes me as unusual about our childhood. We shared a bedroom for fifteen years, we even slept in the same little bed for a long time,' he told the journalist.

I felt sick. There was no mention of their father's violence and perverted behaviour, their mother's endless tears, Dominique's lonely childhood caught between them, all the things that were so obvious the first time I entered the Pelicot house. Joël had always defended his father. He liked to say that if he were ever to travel around the world it would be with him. And now he was publicly heaping blame on his brother as a way of protecting his father again. He could have kept his mouth shut but he felt some need to add his voice to those of the prosecutors. I suppose he thought that this way he would protect his own reputation too. At the end of the article, he said that Dominique had turned into a guy full of hang-ups, who lived beyond his means and had failed to repay any of the large sums of money Joël had lent him over the years.

I closed the wretched magazine. I knew what this meant. The date of the trial had still not been fixed, but it would definitely take place sometime during the next year. My lawyers were working very hard preparing for it. They had met my oldest friends and talked to them about Dominique; they understood that they were going to have to listen to all the memories, even the good ones, if they were to truly understand our relationship. This mattered a lot to me. They had combed through the case file, all the rapists' confessions and denials. They and their colleagues had pored over every minute of the videos, even though it was traumatising and kept many of them from sleeping at night. But, as they told me, it was extremely rare to have such powerful evidence in a rape case. I still refused to watch them.

I couldn't wait for Christmas. Jean-Loup and I were going to stay with David and Céline. Caroline and Pierre would be there too. What I wished for more than anything was simply to be in a place where my life could begin again, with all the little things that matter most. As if we might one day be freed.

But I was trapped in the harsh, blinding light of the films and images I tried to flee, while the rest of the family were suffocating in the shadow and fog into which the revelations had plunged them. We couldn't follow the same path to pull ourselves through. That is no doubt why our wounds did not bring us closer, and why, during the time we spent together, David and Céline never told me about the complaint for sexual assault that Nathan had filed against Dominique in July 2023, just before they joined us on the Ile de Ré. David only told me much later. I felt a dull explosion inside me – another one. I remembered only a present and loving grandfather. For four years, horrible accounts had been falling on me one after the other.

So I placed my hopes in the justice system. I had never asked for anything else – only that it continue its investigation, that it dig, that it give us all some answers. The trial was approaching. Caroline, in turn, was having difficulties with our first lawyer, so I asked Stéphane and Antoine if they could represent her; I wanted her to be well supported. They made contact quickly. It was a way of preparing to face the court together. The date of the first hearing was set for September 2nd.

Time now felt like a countdown.

I wished I could disappear. I wished I didn't have to see or be seen. I wished I could let my lawyers get on with their job and talk on my behalf when the day arrived, behind the doors of a closed hearing. I wished I could send a body double, or at least only a part of me, the part I had not immediately recognised in the pictures that Deputy Sergeant Perret had shown me back in November 2020; the woman known in the media as Françoise. I wished for the whole thing to be over and done with, so I could be left in peace, far from the noise, the crowds, the rumours, the spotlight. I wished for Dominique to spend the rest of his life in prison, and that after the trial none of the others would be released either.

FIFTEEN

The trial, set to begin in Avignon in the autumn, was fast approaching. I thought about it all the time. My two lawyers and I were busy preparing for it. I always referred to them now as 'the boys', an affectionate term that reflected how important they were in my life. They were still unfailingly tactful and reserved with me. In that respect, we were all very much alike.

Stéphane and Antoine had requested that I read the writ of indictment in its entirety. Four hundred pages. A full account of everything I had discovered and been told over the last few years. This time it was not going to be possible to take in the facts bit by bit, as I had always insisted on doing. I was going to have to read it all in one go, the detailed descriptions of how my husband and dozens of strangers had raped me over the course of ten years. Jean-Loup printed the whole thing out for me – I didn't want to read it on a computer screen. I wanted to be able to go through the big sheaf of pages alone, curled up inside or out in a comfortable chair. The account began with a long list of the accused. Their names, occupations, addresses. I highlighted their dates of birth. 1997 . . . 1988 . . . I was born in 1952. Their youth was baffling, and made it all the more appalling. Then, for each one, the facts.

Abhorrent, unspeakably cruel. And entirely absent from my memory, so distant from anything I could imagine, almost unreal, despite being written down in black and white in language that managed to be both vulgar and official. And present throughout, this inert woman, whom they manhandled and dared to describe as consenting.

My stomach tightened. I had to keep putting the pages down to catch my breath. The dates were particularly distressing. I could picture where we were, what had happened before and afterwards, what we were doing then in our lives, what I thought was happiness. That was my birthday. That was the New Year's Eve we'd decided for once to stay in, just the two of us, after the children had gone home. Jean-Loup was reading the pages at the same time. It didn't make me feel uncomfortable. 'How on earth did your body tolerate all this?' he asked me once or twice. Being asked this unanswerable question felt like plunging straight into the horror of what had happened, while at the same time watching it drift away and hearing myself say I had survived. I realised I was ready. Antoine and Stéphane didn't conceal from me the aspect of the trial that was extremely unusual for them too: the fact that there were fifty-one defendants. A pack of rapists. Fifty strangers and the man who was once my husband.

I was impatient to see Dominique in court. The others I feared because of how many they were. I found myself worrying more and more about the closed door of the courtroom, which was supposed to protect me from the prying eyes of the public and the media. I was beginning to realise that a closed hearing meant I would be alone with them. Locked in with them. It was a vague sense I had, difficult to formulate in words. I hadn't discussed it with anyone, but as the trial drew near I kept imagining myself hostage to their gaze, their lies, their cowardice and their contempt. The charges against them were overwhelming, the evidence unprecedented, but the fact remained that there would be fifty-one men gathered in the courtroom. Their voices would be louder than mine. And all their eyes would be on me as they stood shoulder to shoulder, like a wall.

Maybe I was handing them a gift. Maybe I was actually protecting them by asking for the trial to be held behind closed doors. No one would ever know what they had done to me. There would be no journalists present to say their names and describe their crimes. No one beyond those involved in the trial would see their faces, look them up and down and wonder how to pick out the rapists among their neighbours and colleagues, though apparently it is so very easy to recruit them. Perhaps most importantly of all, no woman would be able to enter the courtroom and feel a little less alone; if I hadn't noticed anything, it must surely have happened to others. Apart from the judges, there would be only me, my children and my lawyers, Antoine and Stéphane, facing a horde of men and their forty-five defence lawyers.

I had ardently wanted a closed hearing. I had said it again to the magistrate a few months earlier. It was so clear to me that I hadn't even discussed it with my lawyers. When my previous lawyer had originally suggested having an open hearing as a way of staging a massive public trial of violence against women, I had categorically refused. I did not wish to have my relationship with Dominique exposed to the eyes of the world. I believed that justice must be done but I did not want to be in the spotlight, forever the victim, 'that poor woman' – she wasn't me, and she wasn't the person I wanted to be.

But then, one day in May, I changed my mind. I was walking alone through the forest with the intention of coming back along the beach. The more I walked, the more my doubts grew. If Dominique had been alone in the dock, I would have felt there was no alternative to a closed hearing, but now? A flood of questions filled my head, a strange blend of dread, anger and confidence too, for I was stronger now, no longer the person who had lost everything.

Jean-Loup and I were living together now. The path I was following led back to his house – our house. Just a few months earlier, I was still trying to keep out of the way as much as possible when his children came to visit. On the night of his son's thirtieth birthday, for example, I had planned to spend the evening alone in my little house, until Victor phoned and asked me to join them. He wanted me there.

Most importantly of all, I had my own children back. The summer we had spent together, followed by Christmas and New Year, seemed to have brought us closer. My family was healing. I was happy that we were speaking on the phone more often. I kept up to date with their news, heard the voices of my grandchildren whom I had missed so much. We were each privately dealing with the trial of the father and husband in our own way, but we would be in court together, to seek, if not meaning in all that had happened to us, at least some kind of closure.

I arrived at the beach. The sea air was brisk, it filled my lungs, I felt exposed to the elements, small but utterly alive. I had the physical sensation that I needed the rest of the world. I didn't want to be alone any more. So many strangers had shown me such kindness, made me feel welcome when I had nothing left. I wasn't scared of being seen now, of people knowing. *Shame has to change sides.* The words I'd first heard over a decade ago, a slogan supporting women who had survived rape and domestic violence, came into my head like a refrain, as if tiny blades were honing my thoughts. Everyone needs to see the faces of the fifty-one rapists. They should be the ones to hang their heads in shame, not me. I climbed the dune to a small promontory where the coastal path starts getting steeper, marking the end of my walk and the turning towards Jean-Loup's house. But at the top of the hill I stopped for a moment and gazed into the distance where the sky meets the sea. I knew then that the door to the courtroom had to be opened.

I got home to find Jean-Loup setting the table for lunch. I told him I had decided that I wanted the court proceedings to be open to the media and the public. Very calmly, he replied that it was up to me and he understood. Almost as if he had known it was coming.

After we'd finished eating, I called Stéphane.

'Are you sure, Gisèle?' he asked, astonished at my change of heart.

A little later he and Antoine called me back to ask me to think it over. They gave me a week. But I had made my decision. It liberated me. The next morning I called to tell them I was sure. Straight afterwards I phoned Caroline. She was pleased; she hadn't forgotten that our first lawyer had suggested this nearly four years ago. David and Florian also approved. Of course, none of us could imagine the coming storm – it was impossible to foresee. Nor did I wish for it. We agreed that I would be in court for the first two weeks of the trial, after which my lawyers and their team would speak on my behalf. When I'm struggling, I hide myself away. And it was those bastards I wanted to be put in the spotlight, not me.

Today, looking back on the moment I made the decision, I am aware that had I been twenty years younger, I probably wouldn't have dared request that the case be heard in open court. I would have been too afraid of the looks: those damn looks that women of my generation have always had to contend with; those damn looks that make you waver in the morning between a dress and trousers, that follow you or ignore you, flatter you or embarrass you; those damn looks that seem to tell you who you are or what you're worth, only to forsake you as you age. It was exactly that nerve Dominique pressed when he told me I should be glad my husband still desired me whenever he photographed me coming out of the bathroom. I was, no doubt, still susceptible to it. It's foolish, but that's how we were – freer, more autonomous women, yet still afraid of being abandoned, still longing to be saved. Maybe the shame lifts once you hit seventy and no one looks at you any more. I don't know. I wasn't afraid of my wrinkles or my body. I loved Jean-Loup and he loved me. Happiness was certainly a factor in my decision.

*

'This changes everything, Gisèle,' Antoine and Stéphane told me. 'We shall have to prepare for this in a different way.' They explained that the projection of so many videos of this nature had never occurred before in the entire history of the legal system, and that it was bound to be widely reported and discussed in the media. It was imperative that I watch them beforehand to prepare myself, so that it didn't blow up in my face during the trial.

I hadn't thought of that. I'd imagined I'd be able to leave the courtroom while the videos were being shown, irrespective of whether the trial was held in public. But no, I wasn't going to be able to avoid them. It would be impossible for the public to see them and not me.

So one day I sat down in the study in front of the computer. Jean-Loup sorted out the technical settings, then I asked him to leave the room and made him swear that he would never watch what I was about to see. He closed the door behind him. I knew that he would remain close by in case I called for him.

Stéphane was online from his office in Paris, though I would have preferred him not to be. I'd rather have been alone while I watched them. We switched off our cameras so I could just hear his voice. He would be sending the links to the videos, one by one.

I opened the first one.

I saw a dead woman in darkness.

She was snoring loudly.

I saw her hands were bound.

Her feet too.

'If it's too much, we'll stop,' Stéphane said.

I said I wanted to continue.

He sent another video.

Then another. Each time, he told me what I was about to see.

I saw her mouth forced open. I saw her suffocate and choke. And the husband and the rapist didn't stop.

I saw animals.

I heard them whispering.

I saw a courgette.

I heard Dominique mutter, 'Easy does it.'

I saw him rape me.

Dominique, almighty in the cesspool of the human soul.

My body, the dumping ground of his fantasies.

Punished for what it had refused him. Cast unconscious into the pit of men.

My body tortured.

It wasn't me.

It happened to me, but it wasn't me.

I kept saying that to myself. Not the way I'd said it on that day in Deputy Sergeant Perret's office, when my brain had shut down at what I was being told. Now, my brain was functioning. It remembered nothing of what it saw. It didn't inhabit that body, which was just a shell. My corpse. A doll made of flesh and blood.

I didn't see my life there. They had chased it away, driven it out of my body. I have no idea where it was. Was it hiding under the bed, as I was in the nightmares from long ago that warned me that men would come for me, even in my room?

Or had they destroyed it? Destroyed my life.

Let me go mad.

Killed me.

But no. I was here, alive. Sitting, rigid, in front of the computer. Bystander to my own past, to my own body, filmed by Dominique so he and other men could ejaculate over the body of a woman transformed into a piece of junk.

Now, at last, these images were turning against them.

I knew who I was.

I wanted to see it all. I watched everything that Stéphane had planned to show me. I have no idea how long it took.

I came out of the study. I said to Jean-Loup, 'Don't be upset, I'm going for a walk, I need to be on my own.' I side-stepped his embrace. I didn't want him to hug me. I fled his support, his shoulder to lean on, his kindness, all his attempts to assuage my suffering. I mustn't let it out, I mustn't crack. If I allow the full extent of my pain to be seen, all my pain, I will drown in it. I have no choice but to be invincible.

Jean-Loup watched me go.

Again, I took the path through the forest. Tears rolled down my face. They were dried by the wind, only for fresh tears to flow, and the wind to come back and sting my eyes, sweep away my shame and console me.

It wasn't me.

That woman between sleep and death was not me.

I walked for a long time until I stopped crying. Then I turned and went back home for lunch.

SIXTEEN

It was dusk, the first of September. We were eating pizza in the courtyard of the house Jean-Loup had rented for us in Verquières, ten miles from Avignon. The children were there, as were our lawyers and their colleagues, and it felt as though we were a team. A team that had come together gradually before the summer, as we felt the deadline drawing closer. In June, we'd all gathered again in Antoine's offices on the Champs-Élysées. Antoine and Stéphane had explained that although the indictment did not place us all on the same footing – since it focused on the drugging and rapes I had suffered – the court could nonetheless recognise each of us as victims and allow us to sit among the civil parties during the hearings. I felt relieved to hear it stated so plainly. It mattered to me too. What each of us had endured needed to be acknowledged and heard.

'We're here to support Maman,' David said. It was sweet to hear – words that brought me back to the family we had once been. We were beginning to find within ourselves the strength to face what lay ahead – together. Everything was going to be difficult, the camera lenses and eyes trained on us, the unfamiliar faces, all of it completely alien – except for Dominique, who would be in the dock.

'Do you have any sunglasses, Gisèle?' Stéphane asked. 'You need to shield yourself. You'll be surrounded by cameras.'

The next morning, I put on the only ones I had with me, a cheap pair with round frames that I had picked up from a display stand one particularly sunny day. We made our way from the house to the hotel where my lawyers were staying, then walked together to the Palais de Justice. I was between Stéphane and Antoine, smiling and chatting to break the silence and ease the tension, with the children and Jean-Loup following us. Before long, the building came into sight, a crowd of people and a sea of cameras and microphone booms. Jean-Loup lagged behind. It was important he wasn't seen with us. He was my secret and my future, but now I was walking towards my past.

We were getting close now. As we passed, the cameramen and photographers stood back at a respectful distance.

'Don't look at them,' said Stéphane.

I couldn't see them anyway; everything was a blur. I kept a neutral expression. I let them film the woman who had been subjected to two hundred gang rapes instigated by her husband – the woman I had been trying so hard not to be for the last four years, the woman I couldn't bear to be reduced to, whose face would fill the next day's newspapers and television screens. I didn't look at anyone. I didn't listen. I stepped into the spotlight like a robot, both terrified and determined, my children and my lawyers by my side. I climbed the steps to the Palais de Justice, trying all the while to maintain a protective bubble around myself. The rapid-fire clicking of cameras was followed by the beeps of the electronic security gates, the echoes of our footsteps as we entered the court building, the hubbub of voices. We kept walking. Nobody knew that we were about to request an open hearing. That was the ace up our sleeve. It was my decision, but nevertheless I was afraid. The closer I got to the courtroom, the more terrified I became, but I couldn't let it show.

And then I saw them. The thirty-four rapists who had not been held in pre-trial detention had already taken their seats in the courtroom. Some wore masks, others had pulled hoods over their heads; their names had been made public, and they were simmering with rage. A flock of lawyers in black gowns circled them, presenting a united front with the accused and seeming to take up all the space in the room. Though it was the largest in the building, the courtroom felt very small to me, and there was such a horde of them. As I sat down on the bench reserved for us, they felt uncomfortably close. Not one lowered his eyes. The accused men stared at me defiantly. They would all be pleading not guilty.

Then, under police escort, the men who had been imprisoned since their arrest entered. I watched as Dominique arrived. I saw him before he saw me. Four years had gone by. He looked like a worn-out old man. He walked with a cane and leaned against the glass panel of the witness box as he sat down. He reminded me of Jean Gabin in the role of the convicted murderer in *The Dominici Affair*. As he slowly scanned the courtroom he caught my eye; neither of us looked away. His expression was sombre, heavy with the weight of his confession. He turned his gaze to our children sitting beside me.

Just at that moment Stéphane handed me the document finalising our divorce. All I had to do was sign it, he said. I'd thrown away my wedding ring in Mazan the day after I'd learned the truth, but I would have liked to sign the document together with Dominique, even if that meant going to the prison to do so. I wanted something more solemn to mark the undoing of the day we married.

Dominique's lawyer, Béatrice Zavarro, came over to greet me. 'Don't be too easy on him,' she muttered. It was Dominique speaking through her, recognising his guilt. With that one brief sentence, I understood that the line I had drawn between him and the other accused men had reached into the courtroom. I would not have to confront him in court, because he was going to confess to all the terrible things he had done to me. I hoped to challenge him, interrogate him, listen to the way he answered his daughter's questions, but I would not have to argue with him. With the others, I would.

A piercing bell announced the arrival of the five judges. Everybody stood. Once he had taken his seat and the formalities for opening a trial had been completed, the presiding judge, Roger Arata, turned to me and my lawyers and asked if we wished for a closed hearing. Stéphane rose to his feet and replied that no, his client did not want a closed hearing. Silence fell. All around the courtroom, faces froze in astonishment; the presiding judge's white moustache did not conceal his disapproval of our decision, which went against established convention; the rapists' faces crumpled, then hardened to mirror their lawyers' as they vociferously clamoured for a closed hearing. To our great surprise, the public prosecutor also wanted a closed hearing. Stéphane again stood up to speak, explaining that it was my choice for the proceedings to be held in public and that, according to the law, it was the choice of the victim alone. The judge upheld my decision, the prosecution agreed, and the defence lawyers were left fuming. They were absolutely furious. Stéphane had warned me: they would make me pay for this. I was ready for it.

Stéphane had been to stay with us in July and had asked me to write down the story of my life, my family and my marriage. When I showed him the first draft, he asked me to rework it. 'It's important that everyone understands who you are.' It hadn't occurred to me that anyone would be interested, but I did as he said.

The next thing I had to do was learn how to speak about this in public.

'No, put the papers down, Gisèle, it sounds like you're reciting. You're going to have to address the court without any notes,' he said.

'I won't be able to.'

'Go off somewhere on your own. Try to imagine yourself in that situation.'

How many times had I heard these words over the summer! Stéphane left after a few days – he couldn't stay indefinitely – but I carried on practising without notes, with Jean-Loup facing me in the role of the judge. One day in mid-August I was on a video call with Stéphane, who was in Paris, when the words emerged calmly from my lips – I was talking about the worst days of my life, the hurried departure from Mazan, arriving at the Gare de Lyon – but, at exactly the same moment as always, I began to cry. Stéphane said it would be fine if I broke down during the hearing; everyone would understand I was overwhelmed with emotion.

'No, Stéphane, I don't want to cry. I am not going to cry on the day.'

And I did not shed a single tear on September 5th, the day of my first appearance in court. I talked about being a wife, a happy and fulfilled mother. I talked about the day everything collapsed, the descent into hell when I found out what my husband had put me through. The court knew all that already. I was standing in front of experienced lawyers who had carefully combed through all my interviews with the examining magistrate. But that day I needed to personify my story, to tell it loud and clear, to banish from the courtroom all the ludicrous, abject scenarios that the defence would soon brandish. An army of lawyers was champing at the bit – I was bracing myself. They would suggest that I was consenting, that I was complicit in my husband's games, or simply a drunk. Stéphane sat by my side, ready to prompt me whenever I rushed through something too quickly. I talked about my worsening health, my blackouts, my fear that I was dying, the decade of medical misdiagnoses. It was important not to leave out a single detail. I had to convey my unfathomable shock of that morning of November 2nd 2020 at Carpentras police station, the pain of breaking the news to my children, and the waking nightmare we had been living ever since. I had to make the most of every minute I was granted, because although I was the subject of the trial – the body upon which the crimes had been perpetrated, about to be shown naked on three video screens set up in the courtroom — I was not to be its voice. I had spent the summer practising how to speak in public, but in the end, for the duration of the trial I mostly listened.

I listened to the defence lawyers make a request that the word 'rape' not be used, in order to preserve the presumption of innocence. One proposed 'sexual relations'. One of the judges suggested 'sex scene'. I was fuming inside, but from the bench where I sat, I wasn't allowed to react. I had to restrain myself. All the time. Restrain myself while my lawyers responded. Restrain myself when the presiding judge asked a doctor if my vaginal secretions might be a sign of pleasure. Restrain myself when a female lawyer sneered at a medical examiner testifying to the gravity of my physical condition, 'Oh, let's weep for Madame Pelicot, shall we?' I will not record her name here, nor those of her colleagues, nor those of the defendants. Not out of any consideration for them — their identities are easy enough to find online or in the court records — but so that they will be remembered only for what they are: parrots, deplorable mouthpieces, violent, cowardly little people. I want all that remains of them to be the words they used to trample over me, to reduce one woman — and therefore all women — to absolute submission in the name of male domination.

'I saw a dead woman in the bed. But when I touched her she was warm. I didn't see her face,' one of the defendants said.

'You didn't see her face even when you had your penis in her mouth and she was choking?' the presiding judge asked.

An expert witness testified that this particular scene was so violent I could have died. I don't remember at what point in the trial this exchange took place. But it hardly matters.

'I didn't have time to shop around, so I just went for whatever came up first. I'm not a rapist, but if I had wanted to rape someone, I'd hardly have gone for a fifty-seven-year-old woman, I would have picked a prettier one,' said another.

I listened. It was like being punched.

I had to squeeze past them during breaks in the proceedings. I heard them talking, not even bothering to lower their voices, naturally buoyed by male camaraderie. I saw them high-fiving each other, going to the café across the street at lunchtime, chatting at the bar, buying rounds of beer, laughing. They bonded with each other simply because they were convinced they had done nothing wrong. And yet they didn't resemble one another: some were articulate, others could barely string a sentence together in the witness box; there were old men, bald men, men with paunches, men who were young and athletic; one was constantly chewing gum; another had brought along some policeman friends for support. But they did share one thing: a sense of entitlement. An attitude of complete indifference to whatever anyone said or thought, because power had always been on their side.

Whenever they denied it was rape or claimed they knew nothing about the state I was in, my lawyers requested that one of the videos be shown. The judge described the contents beforehand. Each time I saw Jean-Loup discreetly leave the courtroom. I had made him repeat his promise not to watch them. Whichever of my children were there also stood up and left, as I had asked them to. The judge gave them time to leave the courtroom before turning on the projector. The screens began to crackle. I lowered my eyes, stared fixedly at my phone, flicked through photos of my grandchildren, the sea around the Ile de Ré, even the landscape of Mont Ventoux we could see from Mazan. I took my mind to safe places. But I could still hear the snoring of the heavily sedated woman echo around the courtroom. I was horribly ill at ease, embarrassed that everyone would notice that I snored, seized with shame, the shame of women who are supposed to leave snoring to men, even as I was being tortured on the screen. I could hear the murmuring voices of the accused as they raped me. Ghastly as this was, it was a searing refutation of all the devious falsehoods they had invented for the trial – that they were afraid of Dominique, that under his tyrannical command they had been given no choice.

'Move her leg,' one of them tells Dominique, to make it easier to penetrate the unconscious woman. I remember a few of them sticking their thumbs up. A compliment from the husband: 'Nice one.' So pleased with their performance.

My friend Pascale came and sat down beside me to offer me moral support. She squeezed my arm. I gently lifted her hand and moved it off me. As usual I was shunning the embrace of someone who loved me. She apologised later. I assured her it was fine, I just didn't want to feel her stress on top of my own, or I feared I might drown. I needed to face the situation alone, seated behind my lawyers. At the end of the first week, the children had to return to their lives and their responsibilities. That was unavoidable, of course. But they would be back.

I was dignified, according to the media. The word kept being used to describe me. I don't know if it's accurate, though. It is perfectly reasonable to collapse, and apparently tears can make you feel better. But as I told the judges, I can't cry in public. I am like a Russian doll: inside me are my grandmother in her black mourning clothes, Maman smiling even as she is dying, Papa with all his military stiffness. I hold myself together.

Nonetheless, as the days went by, with all the attacks, insinuations and humiliations, I trembled beneath my armour. I often found myself gripping the edge of my seat. Antoine and Stéphane were right in front of me, but facing the courtroom and focused on reacting when required, so they couldn't help me. We had some respite at lunchtime, when we gathered in a restaurant in Avignon that had become our regular spot. We would prepare for what was coming next, but we also managed to laugh at the preposterous things we'd heard that morning. It was vital, a way to calm our nerves.

I was so happy to get home every evening and to take Lancôme out for a walk in the fields behind our rented house. There was no forest or beach where I could go on long walks any more. And now my face was on television and plastered all over the newspapers the whole time. It was difficult to breathe. Everywhere I went I was that raped woman. I felt invaded, oppressed. I no longer had all the safeguards I had established over the past few years. Fortunately, I did have Jean-Loup, though I knew it was very hard for him too.

We both eventually agreed to accept the assistance offered to us by the Association for Mediation and Victim Support in Avignon. There is one attached to every court, simply providing information or offering concrete assistance. This was how Anne-Sophie Langlet – an incredibly kind young woman who talked and listened, took my mind off the proceedings, and explained the significance of things I didn't understand – came to be sitting next to me in the courtroom. When Anne-Sophie was unavailable, Candice Del Degan, the head of the service, filled in for her so I wouldn't be alone. Both were very familiar with the court's rituals. 'That's normal, part of the game, it's always like that,' Anne-Sophie would reassure me. 'Of course they'll be found guilty,' she promised. She took my hand while the videos were being shown. I let her. When her palm was in mine, I didn't feel my whole life drain away as I did when it was Jean-Loup, or one of my children, or a dear friend. For her, it was a professional act. I was just going through a difficult time.

I can't remember the day I first heard the applause as I walked into the Palais de Justice. I realised that the people around me, mostly women, were forming a guard of honour, something I had never imagined or expected. I could feel the warmth of their bodies, their emotion and vulnerability melding with mine. I think it must have been mid-September, because we had just changed our plans and decided to extend the rental agreement on the house. Our lawyers had cancelled all their other commitments; my family and I had decided to stay in Avignon for the entire trial, which was expected to last four months. We felt we couldn't just be there for the first two weeks and then come back for the summing-up, which had been our original plan.

Something was happening. The story was taking on a magnitude that we hadn't anticipated. Every day more foreign media outlets arrived to cover the trial. I had to embody it, set upright with my presence the tortured body that was being talked about all the time, give it a voice, a face, consciousness, elegance too, all the things that rape seeks to destroy. And more important than anything, there was that crowd of women . . . Morning, noon and night, they queued up in the hope of getting a seat in the overflow room that had been opened to the public. At the end of the day they hung around outside the court building, unwilling to go home, where no doubt plenty of obligations awaited them – food shopping, children maybe, all the things that mean we are constantly run off our feet. But now they seemed in no hurry to return to their daily lives.

The Palais de Justice in Avignon was suddenly at the epicentre of women's suffering. People even addressed letters to me there. Not long after the trial began, I started to be presented with a bundle of correspondence at the end of each day. When we got home Jean-Loup would open the envelopes with a letter opener, and together we would read the stories sent to me by women from all over France. I preferred to read their letters rather than the newspapers; they gave me the chance to listen to the women's voices.

I couldn't stop and greet all the people who came every day to stand outside the Palais de Justice – I had to keep moving, to refrain from talking when I was surrounded by so many cameras and microphones. I kept pace with my lawyers. How could I tell the women waiting to thank me for my courage – when I had no claim to any such thing – that their presence outside the courtroom eased for me what was happening inside, that the long-buried stories they came to lay on the steps were the best possible response to the denial and bravado of the men flexing their muscles inside? I stopped wearing a mask after the first few days, took off my sunglasses to make eye contact, and smiled to let them know I felt less alone with them there. 'No more smiling, Gisèle. We have to focus,' Stéphane murmured, apprehensive and protective. A battle was being waged around how I presented myself. If I smiled brightly, if I wore a new dress, it was immediately used against me by the defence to minimise both the trauma and the crime.

Inside the courtroom, I was gradually getting used to the crowded conditions, the proximity of the rapists, their baleful eyes that seemed to say, 'What do you think you're doing?' I held their gaze. Those men wanted to destroy me. I was going to fight. The cowards' litany resumed, followed by more crackling of the video screens. The images were so damning that the accused had to try to use them to their own advantage in their defence. 'Zoom in on my eyes, you can see I was drugged,' one said. 'Look at my pupils, I only came round when I got into my car,' said another. Both men were incarcerated in the same prison, had the same defence lawyer, and were obviously using the same strategy.

I heard everything. I ended up leaving the room one day

when one of the heavyweights in a black gown pointed out that my pelvis was moving in one of the videos, clear proof that I was conscious, and perhaps even a sign of encouragement. 'I'm going to explode!' I muttered under my breath to my lawyers before exiting the courtroom in protest. I did that only twice in the four months of the hearing.

The defence lawyers were becoming increasingly vehement. They too began demanding that intimate photos taken by Dominique while I was awake – with or without my knowledge – be shown. They were insinuating that I liked it, that I had exhibitionist tendencies, maybe even that I had agreed to be used as bait on the internet. One even went so far as to ask me if I locked the door when I went to the toilet. 'You asked for it, Madame Pelicot!' they would crow vengefully, one after another. It was gruelling, and I wasn't sorry that the trial was open to the public; on the contrary, I realised that it would have destroyed me if no one had been there to hear it all. I told the court that now I understood why many rape victims don't press charges, since so often they end up feeling as if they are the ones being accused. The defence just didn't let up. Sometimes at the end of the day they'd announce a new piece of evidence for the following morning, which would throw the entire case into disarray. And so it was that a defence lawyer promised that a sequence in which I could be heard speaking would be shown the next day, offering irrefutable evidence, he said, of my complicity.

We had no idea which video he was referring to; there were so many that even my lawyers had only watched the many videos that the investigators had selected as incriminating evidence. They noted down the reference. I had to watch it with Antoine that evening, before it was played in the courtroom the next morning. It shows just Dominique and me on the sofa in our living room as I am slowly succumbing to the sleeping pills he had put in my food – he sometimes drugged me for his own pleasure. My body, clothed in a nightdress, slumps, my limbs droop, my eyes are closed, but presumably the sedatives haven't taken full effect, because I grimace as he sodomises me. In a weak voice, I murmur, 'Stop it, you're hurting me.' Hearing myself suddenly brought my tormented body to life. This was the first time I had braved watching the recordings in someone else's presence. When it was over we sat there in silence, but neither of us wanted to be there. We said goodbye. I left the room. Through the window I saw that Antoine hadn't moved. I could tell he was very upset, trying not to cry. Later, he said to me, 'This time, it's you we see on screen. Not a dead woman. You're talking, you say no, you tell him to leave you alone. But Dominique Pelicot takes no notice. It's you he's raping.'

Obviously, the video did not help the defence. But it didn't stop them from trying again. Late one afternoon a request was made for a video of Madame Pelicot performing oral sex on Monsieur Pelicot and actively participating in a threesome to be shown the following morning, proof if it were the case that I was fully aware that my husband was filming. We left the court that day surprised, again wondering which sequence they were referring to. I pre-empted my lawyers' questions: I had never, ever agreed to be filmed by my husband during a sexual act. Jean-Loup and I went to bed perplexed.

Around one in the morning Florian, who had come back to Avignon for a few days, knocked at our bedroom door and told me that Stéphane and Antoine needed urgently to speak to me. I sat up, arranged my pillows behind my back and patted my hair, then opened my laptop. Stéphane and Antoine, their faces drawn with fatigue, informed me that their colleagues Morgane and Adrien had found the two videos. 'Can we show them to you? You must tell us the truth, Gisèle.' A close-up appeared on the screen, exactly what one would imagine. 'Look carefully. Is that you?' Her hair was the same colour as mine. But it wasn't my nose that 'barks at the sky', as one journalist described it. It wasn't my bedroom. Nor was that a picture of my dog in the photo frame. No, that wasn't me. They told me there was another image of the same woman, sitting naked on a swing in our garage in Mazan.

'Go on then, we've come this far, Stéphane. Show me the picture.'

It was definitely our garage. She had the same haircut as me, but her figure was a little fuller, she was younger than me, and she still didn't have my upturned nose. It was a close-up of her stomach that finally convinced everyone: she didn't have a mole above her navel like mine. We were so relieved we burst out laughing, Jean-Loup and me in our bedroom, the two of them in their hotel. What a relief to laugh at the whole situation. We all slept well that night, if only for a few short hours.

In the morning, as every day, the alarm was set for 5.45. I had breakfast and got ready. The more people talked about my elegance – the implication being that a woman who had been so tormented would not have the resilience to care about her appearance – the more attention I gave to what I wore.

The day got off to a comically bizarre start. Before the morning session began, we met in the little side room that was reserved for us. Stéphane wanted to take a photograph of my mole, so I unbuttoned my trousers and lifted my shirt. The videos were shown at the start of the session, but they carried no weight because it had already been established that the woman in the videos was not Madame Pelicot. Dominique had been interrogated and had revealed that the woman who looked like me was called Nadine. She and her husband were a couple of swingers he used to spend time with when I was in Paris looking after our grandchildren. He said that two of the accused, whom he didn't name, were also there in the garage that day.

The woman standing naked and blindfolded on a swing with her hands tied above her head was ultimately the only woman who had freely chosen to appear in the sordid videos he made and distributed. But seeing her offered up like this to the sleazy men around her made it look as if she were destined for abuse too. And it occurred to me once again that Dominique had always had the means to satisfy his urges without resorting to chemical submission, but it had not been enough for him: his obsession was me. I was hoping to hear him admit it.

I was not called to give evidence again until October 23rd. Stéphane offered to stand beside me as he had done the first time, but I told him that I would be fine on my own now.

After six weeks of relentless attacks, I was no longer afraid. I even corrected the judge; I told him that what we were talking about were not 'sex scenes' but rape. I said that it was not a case of 'There's rape and there's rape', as one of the defence lawyers had dared to claim. I said it felt as if I were the one being accused in this courtroom, with fifty-one victims facing me.

It was no problem for me to find the right words. They had been sharpened by the rapists' testimonies, nourished and warmed by the crowd outside that grew larger every day, the crowd of women who escorted me each morning to the entrance of the Palais de Justice. For the last four years I had fled the stifling embraces of my loved ones; I wanted no one's compassion, preferring to rely on my own strength and, no doubt, on my capacity to forget. But this crowd had had enough of forgetting, of the way we are cut out of life and left to suffer alone in unacknowledged pain. This crowd saved me.

It was – and still is, for me – an enveloping, comforting throng. But it also drew attention to a disturbing chain of unacknowledged tragedies, of which we see only the tip of the iceberg, those who came to witness our world on trial. It leaves me with a memory of a few faces that stood out particularly clearly to me and which I will never forget. Like that of the young woman I saw one afternoon as I was leaving the court, tears rolling down her cheeks. She must have been about twenty-five. As I passed, I heard her say that she could never be as brave as me. I stopped. I had to speak to her. By chance there were no cameras or microphones following me, so I went up to her and said she mustn't cry, or I would too, and I needed to stay strong. With a finger I gently wiped the tears away from under her eyes.

It was that young woman – her terror, her youth – I was thinking of when I addressed the court midway through the trial. I had prepared some notes, in which I had jotted down words that I was using for the first time in my life: 'Every day people thank me for my courage. I want to tell them this is not courage, but a deep urge and determination to change our patriarchal, sexist society.' These were words I would never have uttered before.

SEVENTEEN

'Monsieur Pelicot, you're not watching the videos?' the presiding judge asked one day.

'No, I'm worried I'll still find them pleasurable to watch. I have a lot more work to do on myself with the psychologists.'

He sat alone in a glass-panelled box, in a large armchair that he was allowed to use because of hip pain, on a platform that gave him a slightly elevated position. This reinforced his role as the ringleader he had once been. He even set himself up as an accuser assisting the prosecution: each time one of his former acolytes denied all responsibility for raping me with the excuse that he had been trapped, or even denied that it was rape at all, Dominique would interrupt him to reassert with authority that his accomplice had come of his own volition, knowing exactly what he was going to do. In relation to the crimes against me, Dominique admitted everything. He even recognised that he still felt aroused on viewing the atrocities he'd inflicted on me.

I still chose not to watch the videos when they were shown in court. But I hadn't forgotten how sadistic and terrifying my husband looked in that footage, I hadn't forgotten those indelible images I had seen once, just once: his hand supporting my limp neck to help one of the rapists forcefully penetrate my mouth, or his fingers, on which his wedding ring still glinted, guiding a stranger's penis into my vagina.

I still wished I could speak to the man sitting across from me in the courtroom. We had spent a lifetime together, but all I had left of him by this stage were his confessions, his eyes avoiding the images that still excited him even now, and a faint hope for the rehabilitative therapy he'd started in prison.

Had that man ever really existed?

That was one of the central questions of this trial. An essential one for me. We are made up of our memories. And neither the four years that had gone by nor the scale of the barbarity revealed to me had erased mine. What was I to do with them? What meaning should I give them? During the first few days in court, I watched my children enter the witness box and pour out their rage and sorrow. It tore me apart. I felt keenly how alone we were, how difficult it was going to be for us to heal. Contrary to what people might think, unhappiness does not bring people together. Dominique had devastated us all, isolated and propelled us away from each other. My heart tightened as I listened to David talk about the relationship he had once had with his father, all the good times they'd shared, and now his profound sense of betrayal and disgust; to Caroline, as she portrayed an affectionate father, a considerate man she had felt very close to, then declared that he was nothing more to her now than the worst sexual predator of the last twenty years; and to Florian, almost hoping publicly that he was someone else's son, that he didn't have the same blood in his veins as his mother's tormentor, that he didn't carry the same genes as the worst of men.

The expert witnesses were then called to give evidence. That day in September had been scheduled to deal solely with Dominique. However, he only appeared for a few minutes at the beginning of the session – just long enough for his lawyer to explain that he needed to go to the hospital to have his kidney stones treated. He vanished, as if he preferred to be absent when we were talking about him. My lawyers asked the psychiatrists the question that had been haunting me: 'What kind of personality allows someone who claims he loves his wife to inflict these scenes on her, to participate in her debasement, to put her in danger? How can this unfathomable contradiction exist in one man?'

The psychiatrist Paul Bensussan, who had conducted a lengthy evaluation of Dominique, spoke of a man split in two. He explained that different and opposing personalities can coexist inside one individual – one personality connected to reality, the other to his fantasies. Like day and night, I thought. 'He may have been sincere in how he presented himself,' he added.

Sincere. I clung to that word. It let me keep part of my life, as if it gave a little credit to my memories.

As Dr Bensussan continued with his report, he described a man completely lacking in empathy, a narcissist who had developed virtually every form of sexual paraphilia: a taste for dominant–submissive relationships, voyeurism, sadism, necrophilia, fetishism, and candaulism as well – the practice of achieving arousal through watching or exhibiting images of one's partner having sex with another. He added that the split in Dominique's personality was so pronounced that any kind of authentic introspection would be difficult for him.

What did this clinical assessment leave me of the man I had known? Had he died long ago? And if so, when? After ten, twenty or thirty years of marriage? Had he ever in fact existed? Those were the questions this trial kept whispering to me.

Sometimes I switched off and let the experts' words rise and float away in the courtroom. It was humiliating to listen to their dissections of my life, my mind and my body. As the proceedings went on and one after the other medical and psychological experts gave evidence, I heard discussions of my age, of women of my generation, of my average IQ, of the number of my orgasms; I heard detailed descriptions of each of my orifices, its colour and secretions, as if I were laid out before the whole assembly, as well as appearing naked and unconscious on the screens. Paul Bensussan talked about 'the wife' and her 'unimaginable blindness'. Which shouldn't be taken as a sign of guilt, he added, nor as evidence of complicity, as some of the defence counsel suggested. 'In a way, the other person can split along with the splitter,' he concluded. What was that supposed to mean? That I had been blind to the alarming signals that Dominique and his dangerous double personality must have displayed? That I'd been incapable of protecting myself and my children?

From where I was sitting, I would often observe the women accompanying the defendants – mostly their partners, wives or exes, but sometimes their mothers or sisters too. These women were suffering. I could sense their fragility, the violence inflicted on them. They were prisoners in a room where the judges demanded that they reveal everything about their private lives, under the watchful eyes of the accused insisting on their unfailing support. One mother said no, my son is incapable of doing such a thing. She was about to be subjected to a video of her child raping a woman her own age. She chose to leave the courtroom, as all the women did. They all left. None of them wanted to be confronted with those images, to be forced to watch their loved one as he was committing rape. One wife talked about how when her mother was ill, she refused to have sex with her husband, and said that 'as a man, he had to go looking elsewhere for it'.

I asked my lawyers to say something to her, so she wouldn't be left feeling that it might have been her fault. 'Madame Pelicot would like you to know that she believes you hold no responsibility whatsoever for what your husband has done,' Stéphane said. I could have been that woman.

I had felt so guilty after my affair – that phase of my life that was exhaustively analysed in court as a possible turning point for Dominique – so guilty about causing him pain. And I'd given him the freedom to have affairs of his own afterwards, convinced that I was in the wrong and that he deserved sexual partners who were more liberated. I knew what that woman was going through. I had been that woman, who placed her man's satisfaction before her own. I'd forgotten the new sensations, the pleasure that I'd found in my escapade with Didier, the feeling that I could at last let myself go in his arms. There was never any future for Didier and me, but simply less tension – the tension Dominique instilled in all our sexual relations, in which I was constantly forced to set boundaries.

I had never questioned those boundaries; I had let him transform them into grievances. According to him, my limitations, my blockages and my prudish nature meant I couldn't give him everything he wanted. I had never allowed myself to examine what frightened me: was it sexuality or was it him? Even when Dominique was arrested, the terror I felt at the discovery of what he'd done hadn't prevented me from feeling the familiar guilt rise up inside me again. What could I have done differently to help him overcome his demons? But that was all over now. It was not my fault, and it never had been. I now understood what kind of serious pathology I had been wedded to. These four long years had helped. My new life, my relationship with Jean-Loup, had too.

I was no longer afraid.

But the fact remained that the procession of women who came to give evidence held up a mirror to the person I had once been. It reflected nothing more than the inner conflict we all feel, the wars we wage against ourselves. When their partners had been arrested, the police had offered to test the women's hair, concerned that they might have been victims of the same practices as I was. All of them refused. Never, that was impossible. They all trusted their men. Despite the fact that Dominique loved to convert others to his modus operandi.

That was how Madame Maréchal was drugged and raped by both her husband and mine approximately ten times. In the witness box, she spoke about how she had believed she was happy, just as I had; she talked about their modest and fulfilling family life with five children, and then about the day when she woke up to find Dominique in her bed. He had escaped through the window. Monsieur Maréchal had blathered some story about allowing a voyeur who liked underwear into the house, but Dominique had in fact come to rape her.

I wasn't in court the day she took the stand, because her husband hadn't assaulted me, and I wasn't entirely tied to that part of the case. My lawyers, worried to see me already so tense and exhausted barely into the second week of this marathon trial, had told me my presence wasn't essential and advised me to take a few hours to breathe and rest. So I hadn't heard her testimony. I regret that, because this woman had been raped by my husband. She didn't press charges against either him or her own husband. The next day, I was cross-examined about my lack of reaction to these revelations by the defence, who were always eager to prove my duplicity or my weakness towards Dominique. I replied that Madame Maréchal was within her rights to act as she saw fit, that it wasn't for me to judge her. And when Monsieur Maréchal's family came to give evidence and talked about his childhood – how he was forced as a boy to watch his father and other men rape his mother, how he was tied to a tree and beaten, how he was regularly subjected to corporal punishment, how he saw his father leering at his sisters and how he performed fellatio on his father in order to protect them – I felt once again that I could have been Madame Maréchal.

*

'I'm no worse than my father,' Dominique said one day, about a month into the trial. I had been expecting to hear that. It was not minimising his crimes to see them as an echo of his childhood – the shadow of his tyrannical father, the constant tears of his mother. It was not beside the point to remember that young Nicole had been abused, or that his half-sister, Geneviève, had been so harassed that she had chosen to leave home at seventeen. Geneviève came in person to give evidence. Over eighty years old, frail and breathless, she told the court how her stepfather, Denis, had terrified her. But then it was Joël's turn to testify. He made his entrance into the courtroom with all the poise of a local dignitary. He acknowledged that Denis had raped Nicole, but according to him this was a trivial detail, an unremarkable occurrence, the fate of countless girls who were wards of the state and caught in similar traps.

No, he said, his father was a decent man. His half-sister was making things up. Likewise, he asserted that Dominique had concocted the story about being raped by a male nurse when he was eight. Joël recounted the episode as if it had happened only yesterday. The day his brother came home from the hospital, their father had shown the family the Formica table and chairs he'd just bought, and told young Dominique he would only be getting the stool, given what he'd cost them in medical expenses. According to Joël, Dominique then revealed what the nurse had done during the night on the general ward. Their parents had called the hospital, who denied any wrongdoing. Joël told the court that he believed his brother had been a compulsive liar since his early childhood.

Dominique raged from his glass box. 'Our parents never knew what happened! I never said a word to anyone about it when I came home. There was no way I could talk about it... Our father was the first to wreck the family. As for me, I accept what I did and will pay for it. But our father never paid the price for what he did.'

I was restless in my seat. The state prosecutor, who was sitting close to me, said, 'I sensed you were upset when your brother-in-law gave evidence.'

'Yes, I was. He was lying.'

I had a clear memory of that Formica furniture; it was still in their kitchen when I became part of the family. I remembered Dominique's mother sitting slumped on one of the chairs, as he begged her to leave his father. And this courtroom was where all that violence was culminating, where that chain of fear had led. The man who had seen those horrors, denounced them, and even fled them, carried them within him more than anyone else – and had become a criminal. He had far surpassed his father's horrors.

For fifty years, I had believed the exact opposite: that we were saved, that we had a good life. I was wrong. And now I was attending the autopsy of our relationship in the large courtroom of the Palais de Justice in Avignon. 'When Dominique Pelicot met his wife, she didn't heal him, she reconciled him with himself,' his lawyer, Béatrice Zavarro, said. Though she was representing Dominique, she was extremely gracious to me throughout the trial.

Sometimes Dominique made discreet signs to me from his box. He put his hand over his heart. I did not respond. Was that the gesture of the man I had once thought I knew? I let him fall into the void he had hurled us all into. I was under fire from the defence lawyers who accused me of supporting and protecting Monsieur Pelicot. One, a woman, said that I was always staring at him, another added that I was 'not being transparent'. But I was absolutely not protecting Dominique. His fate was cast, he could not commit any more crimes – not against me, or anyone else.

I was simply protecting our memories, parts of our life, our story. Sometimes, after a house fire, a few walls are left standing; though blackened and burnt they are still there, perhaps showing the outline of an old staircase, a pattern of wallpaper that needed changing, or a trace of footsteps and moments of togetherness. That was how it appeared to me in my mind; I was looking for a few relics among the ashes. I couldn't face losing everything. I was fighting to keep those walls standing, to stay upright myself. If the last fifty years of my life were taken away from me, it would be as if I had never existed. I would be dead.

Among the ruins of our life, there were those two photographs of Caroline asleep, taken without her knowledge or consent. She spoke about them when she first addressed the court, about how afraid she was that she'd been drugged and raped too. There were also the nauseating montages of my daughters-in-law in the shower, taken with a pen camera hidden in the bathroom. Dominique had cut the pictures up and used the bodies, pasting the images between two men or under a photograph of his own erect penis. His abhorrent fantasies had crept into every room in our house.

The psychiatrist explained that the love Dominique Pelicot felt for his family was not, in itself, a sufficient barrier to rule anything out. He raised the question of incest, which seemed to leach out from the images and photomontages Dominique had made. The question lingered throughout the trial. It was not the matter at hand but we were still hoping for answers. In that solemn legal setting, we laid bare all our wounds and what was left of our lives. Caroline repeatedly telephoned the lawyers, both ours and her father's, begging them time and again to ask the question, because she was sure that her father would end up cracking. Our house was still burning.

Antoine, who was representing Caroline and Florian, asked Dominique, 'Why can't you at least admit to having once looked at your daughter in an incestuous way? This is starting to be too much for her to bear . . .' Dominique persisted in saying no, against all the evidence of the photographs and montages. He continued denying that he had taken the photographs, even though they had been stored in a file on his hard drive.

'I never looked at her like that,' he kept repeating. His lawyer solemnly asked him whether he had ever felt the slightest temptation to touch his children or his grandchildren. Dominique, his voice choking, swore he had never put his grandchildren in danger, and, turning to Caroline, said,

'Caroline, I never touched you. I never drugged or raped you. You can't say that. It's impossible, I never did that.'

She was sitting beside me that day. I wasn't asking her to believe her father. How could she? He had told us so many lies. And if I still sometimes tried to find, in the split man the psychiatrists had described, the man who loved his children, Caroline had no reason to do the same. But I was at least hoping that she would hear and take to heart what the examining magistrate, Gwenola Journot, had said when she declared to the court that her investigation of the possibility that Caroline had been raped by her father had reached a dead end. There was no further evidence to support the allegation: no other images, no videos, no messages. Caroline didn't have any physical symptoms or hazy memories of ever having been sedated. There was no time when she had been alone with her father. There were just those disgusting images of her that had become an obsession for us all.

We did not discuss the magistrate's statement afterwards. We couldn't. Caroline was constantly losing her temper with the lawyers, with Jean-Loup, with her husband. This trial could not ease her pain, nor dissipate our doubts, nor answer the questions that were torturing us all. Worse still, it risked putting even more distance between us, for the judges were focusing only on the facts and evidence in the case being prosecuted, and therefore on my ordeal, leaving Caroline with the sense that she was being overlooked. 'My mother was raped, yes, under the influence of drugs, yes. The only difference between my mother and me is that in her case there is proof. For me, it's an absolute tragedy,' Caroline said in court. That 'yes' she repeated felt like a blade to me; she was cutting her pain from mine, setting the two in opposition. I had no idea how to respond or how to reassure her, since reassuring her now meant betraying her.

I wanted the truth, the whole truth. I wasn't trying to save appearances, nor spare the wife and mother I had been, that woman who had seen nothing, who either had not been able to protect her family or hadn't known how to. That wife and mother was lying almost dead on the three screens in front of us, and on another in the room next door – an additional space open to the public, barred to minors, and where the faint of heart were advised to leave. I was wrung out. I occasionally put on my sunglasses inside the courtroom to hide my tears. What was happening in there was infinitely sad, while outside the court a strong and liberating wind was rising.

I wanted to leave. To go home. For the trial to continue without me. So many times I was tempted to go back to my island. But there were all those messages I kept receiving, that crowd, the women waiting for me outside the courtroom whom I could not disappoint. Just as I could not concede a victory to the rapists and their defenders. To leave would mean becoming a deserter. Stéphane and Antoine recommended I seek medical advice. Anne-Sophie from the victim support service arranged an appointment with a psychiatrist at Montfavet hospital in Avignon. She was a trauma specialist who had worked with the victims of the terrorist attacks in Nice. It was strange to hear the connection being made between terrorism and intimate-partner violence, but who knows, maybe we had something in common after all. I saw the psychiatrist three times: she tried to help me summon back my strength, that old suit of armour that it seemed so many parties involved in the trial were reproaching me for wearing. It did me good to see her. It felt like retracing my steps.

One day, when the court session had been shorter than usual, Jean-Loup and I took the opportunity to go back to the Leclerc supermarket in Carpentras. I asked to see the security guard who had discovered Dominique upskirting women and had set everything in motion. The manager took us to a back room, where the walls were covered in screens connected to the security cameras. The security guard was moved, I could see it at the corners of his blue eyes. I was too. We hugged. That man had saved my life. He told me he was also living in Mazan at the time, and that he'd gone into hiding when the scandal first broke because he'd received threats in the village. It was home to several of the rapists, some of whom had not yet been identified.

I hoped the men who had threatened him were now among the accused in the courtroom. I expected nothing from them. From Dominique, I had looked for more than a litany of apologies, at least the beginnings of an explanation – though it never came. 'I am a rapist. I have to face the fact and deal with it,' was all he said. He spoke in a voice that was weaker and more weary than I remembered but had lost none of its authority. And even though he was the one being judged, he showed icy composure. When Stéphane and Antoine had asked him how he could have put me in such danger when he claimed to love me, he replied, 'I regret being naive.'

'Naive?' Stéphane repeated. What was that gentle word doing there, when everything on the screens was so barbaric and violent? Dominique had nothing to add.

I was the one who had been naive.

During Dominique's final cross-examination, he declared that he had wanted to 'force an insubmissive woman into submission'. What was he talking about? About my refusal to let him photograph our lovemaking? About anal sex? About that evening in 2012 when we went to Pontault-Combault with a couple of insistent friends, who were determined to see what the local swingers club was like because they knew the boss? I had refused at first, but they wouldn't take no for an answer – we could just go and have a drink, they said, and it's true, we did go and drink a glass of champagne at the bar while watching people shimmying on the dance floor. There was a door leading to other rooms. Dominique had gone to have a look but had come back quickly, and I'd asked to go home while our friends stayed on. I knew he wanted us to go in. 'You go, but without me,' I said to him afterwards, preoccupied as always with his satisfaction. He probably did go back to the club alone, but I now realise that the whole point was to go with me.

I had been the key to his escape, but he expected me to be the plaything of his expanding fantasies. In the end I was punished for saying no. Our bedroom, which he'd opened up to strangers, was an extension of that place I had declined to set foot in. The lingerie I was wearing in the videos was exactly the kind I had always refused to buy. Drugging me, inducing my chemical submission, was his response to my refusals. The man I had believed I was in a relationship with for the past five decades was not in this courtroom.

And yet I felt the need to talk to Dominique one final time. So many questions had been swirling around in my mind since I had walked out of the police station alone four years ago. On the day I addressed the court for the last time, those questions had coalesced into a single one that seemed to hang over our memories, our relationship, our youth, over the birth of each of our three children, over our family holidays, our intimacy, our travels, our troubles too: in the name of all that we had lived through together, how could he have done this?

It was a question with no answer. I had finally come to understand that. But I asked it anyway that day in court, without turning to face Dominique, as Stéphane had instructed me: 'Look at the presiding judge, not at him, otherwise you'll crack.' I asked the question in order to be able to look back and not see complete darkness, the abyss into which Dominique had plunged us.

Of the last days of those three months of the trial, I remember only fragments, seemingly contradictory messages, shadow and light. This trial would be the trial of rape culture, Antoine declared in his closing statement; it would be a testament left for future generations, Stéphane said in his. But I knew that whatever the court decided, it would never be enough to account for the loss and devastation in each one of us. My children and I remained just as isolated as we had been at the beginning of the proceedings.

'You always used to say Maman is a saint – well, you were the devil,' Florian said, glaring at his father.

Caroline walked as close as she could to the glass box in which her father sat, and demanded a confession. 'I never touched you, I never touched my children!' he shouted.

'You're lying! You'll end up alone like a dog!' she cried.

Before the judges retired to consider the verdict, the accused were given a final chance to speak.

Dominique said that he would accept his prison sentence, but that he could never truly pay the price for the harm he had inflicted on his family.

Monsieur Maréchal requested he be given a life sentence.

Some of the rapists asked for my forgiveness. I refused to grant it. None of them had alerted the police to what was going on in our house, none of them had tried to help me.

I heard lots of apologies. And lots of 'I have nothing to add'.

Dominique was sentenced to the maximum twenty years in prison. I felt neither joy nor pain. It was over. I still had some way to go before understanding what had happened, or accepting that I never would understand it. In the wording of the verdict, he was also found guilty of recording and disseminating images of a sexual nature of his daughter and his two daughters-in-law.

All the accused were found guilty of rape, or of attempted rape and aggravated sexual assault. None of the men who had sullied me, none of the men who had touched a woman without her consent, would avoid a prison term. The battle was won.

Very early in the morning on the day the sentences were handed down, I received a phone call from Laurent Perret, the police officer from Carpentras. He told me he would be there as I came out of the courtroom. 'It will be an honour for me to ensure your safety,' he said. I was calling him Lieutenant Perret, getting the ranks muddled up. In fact, I never knew exactly what my father's rank was either, and I had naturally promoted the man whose voice had turned my life upside down. Since then, I've learned how hard he found it to talk to me, how he had spent days and nights before our first meeting wondering what words to use when he summoned me to the police station. He knew he was going to hurt me. He had saved me.

And there he was, with his police colleagues, as I exited the courtroom. He cleared the way for me through the crowd with his broad shoulders. The throng was so dense that I couldn't see my feet. I said a few words to the press, with my grandson Nathan at my side, first for my children, grandchildren and daughters-in-law, who have all suffered lasting damage and whom I wish I could have protected, then for all the unrecognised victims, whose pain I could read in the eyes of the women surrounding me, or in their letters. I ended by declaring that I had no regrets about opening the courtroom doors and making the trial public – it was now up to society as a whole to address these issues, and to change.

Outside the Palais de Justice a doughty women's chorus had broken into song. A banner with 'Merci Gisèle' had been unfurled and was floating from the crenellated battlements of Avignon. It was all too much for me. Now I was no more than a reflection, the object of public discussion, an image, an icon even, for some people. I was exhausted. I lost sight of my children and grandchildren in the tussle outside the courtroom. I was afraid of the after-effects this trial would have on us, but I was happy it was over now, that life could move on, and without knowing whether I was walking or being carried by the crowd, I felt myself being pushed into the back of the car with Stéphane and Antoine. Jean-Loup was behind the wheel. We set off.

EIGHTEEN

This story is no longer just about me. It has roused a deep, silent pain as old as time. It has sparked an extraordinary seismic shift. How to make sense of what has happened, of what my ordeal has unleashed? All those women who write to tell me they have finally found the strength to speak out, to face up to their struggles, in some cases to divorce their husbands, all those thousands of letters; the man I met on a train platform who thanked me on behalf of his two young daughters; the teenage girls on the other side of the world who recognised me beneath Rio de Janeiro's monumental statue of *Christ the Redeemer* and came up to me with tears in their eyes; the couple I met on the dunes not far from my house who told me they loved me. I smile and thank them, tell them I love them too, try to tamp down the overflowing admiration in their eyes. All I've done is pick my way along the fault line that runs through me.

When I was sixteen, I thought constantly about my purpose in life. At that age, it's normal to wonder what it's all about. But I had a yearning for something more; I wanted a mission. That was what I needed in order to escape the sadness that had engulfed my family and might well have destroyed me too. It was 1968, and women were coming together so they could fight to break free from a life mapped out for them, to fight for the right to abortion, for their liberation. I heard them, admired them, but was far removed from them. I couldn't really grasp what this conflict between men and women was all about. I was haunted by the melancholy figure of my father who, like my brother, I had never been able to console. I had never been able to do anything for these two taciturn men, utterly devoted to Maman and lacking any sort of masculine brutality. I dreamed of love, of marriage, of having a family of my own that would make everything right, that would give me back what had been taken away. I yearned for the chance to grow old and grey alongside a man, holding my children close as they grew bigger and then began to wriggle free, gently shrugging off their mother's embrace. I wanted all that; nothing could make me change course, and I believed I had committed myself to it by marrying, as they say, for better or for worse.

And here I am, in my seventies, a martyr, the symbol of a new feminist wave that I hardly know a thing about. This time I won't turn away from it. I will stay as I am, without hatred, unable to set men against women, for I believe we are meant to live side by side. I imagine this might disappoint a few campaigners. I am not a radical person; all I've ever wanted is a conventional, quiet life. But I heard women transforming the pain of the trial into emancipatory chants that they sang on the steps of the Palais de Justice. I heard joy and anger prevailing over silence, and I am more than happy to offer my experience as an example and my name as a battle flag. It fills me with relief to think that a woman who wakes up, unable to remember what happened the night before, might think of me – or rather my story. Yes, I prefer to put it like that: she will think about what happened to me. I don't like the status of victim, and I have never felt like an icon. Perhaps I actually did fulfil the sense of mission that haunted me when I was sixteen.

I have lived a thousand lives. I really felt this one day a few months after the trial, as Jean-Loup and I were walking along Tahiti beach in Brittany, where my parents once left fleeting footprints in the sand, and where I used to picnic in summer with my father, brother and stepmother. In fact it was because of this churlish, unpleasant woman that I found myself back in Brittany. She was about to turn ninety-eight. I had stayed in touch, as I had promised my father on his deathbed I would, and I suppose also because that is part of who I am. I find it hard to break ties, I need an anchor to hold on to the past, and all I had left was this old woman who had never loved me, not even a little. I'd called her after my life had fallen apart. I told her that Dominique had died of a heart attack. It was easier than telling the truth. But, as the case gathered momentum, I changed my story – not very hard to do with a woman of that age – and said he was in prison for rape, though I didn't give her the details, his terrifying methods, everything I had suffered. I was still afraid of her hurtful responses, her callous insensitivity. I had not forgotten the privations and humiliations she had inflicted on my brother and me. And now I had come to introduce Jean-Loup to her.

She'd told us before we arrived how much lunch at the nursing home would cost, and we had promised to pay our share. As we sat through the unpalatable meal, I listened to her boasting to Jean-Loup about how well she had trained me, and complaining that my mother's grave had cost more than the one in which she would soon be joining my father. Nothing, absolutely nothing, could mellow her. But I was used to biting my tongue and I even had my photo taken with her after lunch with my hand resting on her shoulder.

Six months later, the picture lay on her coffin. It had been cropped so that only she remained, but my hand was still on her shoulder: my hand trapped in the image as if trapped in my childhood; my hand that might make it seem as if this woman had loved and been loved; my hand, too docile, suggesting affection where there was none, still full of kindness even towards those who had hurt me. A chapter of my life was closing for good. Only Jean-Loup and I were there to accompany the body to the cemetery; not one member of her family had come. In the cemetery, I looked down into the open grave towards my father, who had wished to be buried elsewhere, and I smiled at him, as if to say, *You see? I came. I kept my promise.* But what promise? Always to do the right thing, say nothing, smooth things over? My smile had not kept me safe.

Sometimes I wonder whether we might have had more self-confidence if my father had married a kinder woman, even if she probably wouldn't have made up for the loss of our mother. Perhaps my brother would not have sunk so deep into sadness that his heart eventually stopped beating altogether, and I would not have thrown myself so rashly into love. In my desire to be saved, I rushed headlong into the wrong relationship. I could go on rewriting this story for ever . . . If only Maman had not fallen ill, we would not have moved back to the Indre, and I would never have met Dominique. But what's the point of going in search of a life I never had, trying to pinpoint the moment I took a wrong turn? I understand only too well the sequence of events that led to our first meeting, which was so powerful that I found myself talking about it in the office of Deputy Sergeant Perret as if it had been just the day before. There's no point getting lost in regret.

I suppose that's why I decided to brave the court. Everyone was expecting to see a wreck of a woman arrive. But that was not what happened. I still knew why I had been in love with Dominique and, as I told the court, I will probably spend the rest of my life puzzling through my memories in order to salvage a few good ones. I will never be reduced to my tortured body; that is not where my soul is, it's not who I was as a girl, nor is it the woman I have become. It is strange to think of me before, me today, to superimpose one on top of the other. I know how alike they are, the life force they share, but I know their differences too. I am no longer the wife in shock at the police station and I am no longer the woman I was before I discovered Dominique's true nature. I am moving forward.

What I needed was to walk. I needed the silence, though it is not that easy to cope with. It is a constant effort. I shall see it through to the end. I am uncomfortable with tears and public displays of emotion. I refuse to let myself be carried away by hatred. If I seem a little stiff behind my smiling mask, dignified to some, suspect to others; if I seem, even in my children's eyes, to have fallen short, given the horrors that were uncovered, it is because I am focusing on the next step, the next day. It's like walking a tightrope – I simply have to keep going. I know the feeling of the void all too well; I have lived under its threat all my life, it stalks me, takes away all that is dear to me. It was the void that yawned before me when I lost everything, the day I found myself with my two suitcases and my dog in the jostling crowd at the Gare de Lyon. I recognised its draw. I could have collapsed, but I chose to hold on, promising myself, yet again, that life can also go on. It was the best I could offer my loved ones.

And yet my relationships with both David and Caroline grew increasingly strained in the aftermath of the trial. Nathan's complaint was dismissed. The unanswered questions continued to drive a wedge between us. Doubt, Antoine warned, risked condemning Caroline to a never-ending hell. I could not be prouder of her for setting up the charity M'endors pas, Don't Put Me Under, to take action against domestic chemical submission. I hope that by taking up this courageous fight against a largely unacknowledged, barely imaginable phenomenon, by launching a campaign to raise awareness and engaging in dialogue with government bodies, she too will find her mission in life. Of course, I am only too aware that public discussion cannot erase private suffering, that once we are alone the past resurfaces in each of us, and that my daughter, in her woman's body, is haunted by a horrific, tragic experience. I find it harder to understand the violent words, the laying bare of our problems. But I'll wait. I'll wait as long as it takes for things to calm down – precisely because I believe in the power of memory, in the mark it leaves on us, in the infinite love I have given and received from my children.

By the time I had to go back to court on October 6th 2025, to the Court of Appeal in Nîmes, the banners were back up and the feminist anthems were being sung once more. But returning, revisiting the case, re-entering the courtroom, hearing it all repeated over and over, tied me up in terrible knots. I could not bear to relive it. And yet I had to. Of the seventeen defendants who had begun the appeal process against the original verdicts, only one had ultimately gone through with it. The fact that even one of them was still prepared to demand that he be acquitted, that a single night of my torture, June 28th 2019, might escape being classified as rape, was unbearable. I had to be there. Florian was by my side; he did not want me to be alone. There was no longer a horde of men facing me – just one man hunched in his seat who refused to admit that he had raped me, who kept repeating that he had been set up and had never intended to hurt me.

'What is rape?' the judge asked him.

'It's when someone is tied up and forced to have sex,' he said. 'But I didn't use any violence.'

His answer was steeped in grotesque male entitlement. The year that had gone by since the first trial had not forced him to reflect on what had happened, just as it had not stifled the sniggers and comments that can still be heard in the outside world; even among supposedly thoughtful people, apparently there are still those who don't entirely believe me. We should ask all these idiots with their millennia-old misogyny the question that the judge enunciated slowly and clearly, the way one would to a child:

'Did she act in the way that a woman does when she agrees to it?'

'No,' the defendant conceded.

Once again, the fourteen videos in which he appears had to be shown. At my request, Florian left the courtroom. Morgane, Stéphane's younger colleague, slipped me a medallion to squeeze, and I lowered my gaze, but it was easy to tell who my attacker was: the man craning his neck up towards the screen, fascinated by the spectacle of his sexual vigour, so fascinated that he didn't seem to understand that his behaviour was likely to increase the sentence he was appealing. Stéphane and Antoine both gave him several opportunities to acknowledge his crime, bearing in mind that, as Stéphane so aptly put it, I had not come to seek his downfall. I was not insensitive to the relatives of the accused, who were all suffering anew. 'Gisèle Pelicot is simply asking that you do not dispute what she went through, a rape that has made such an impression, a rape that is striking because of its total absence of humanity, like all rape,' said Stéphane. 'Did you rape her?'

'No,' insisted the rapist. We began to wonder what we were all doing there.

One afternoon Dominique was called as a witness. He said that the defendant had not been coerced and that he had 'enjoyed it'. Those were the words he used. He remained seated while he spoke, because his hip was still causing him pain. Not once did Florian, beside me, take his eyes off him; he glared unflinchingly at the father whom he said he had always feared. Dominique's authoritarian presence had not waned, even after a year in solitary confinement. 'I have the kind of personality that people either like or loathe,' he admitted, and everyone understood what he meant from the way he took control of the proceedings in the courtroom. 'We lived together for fifty years. For forty years, my behaviour was impeccable – for ten years, it was despicable. After forty years, she trusted me – she couldn't see the devil right in front of her. I did everything I could to make sure she saw nothing,' he said.

Later Florian observed that it was he who had first used the word 'devil' to describe his father and that Dominique now used it. This was clearly not a coincidence. He was talking to us. But his peculiar accounting of our life together is false. Forty years of impeccable behaviour, when he had confessed to attempted rape in 1999? And remains a suspect in the still-unsolved 1991 murder case? His lawyer's request that the body be exhumed was initially rejected by the court on the grounds that after so many years a sample would reveal nothing, as the victim's bones would now only yield her own DNA. But it was later ordered by the Court of Appeal. So it will happen – and it will be a dreadful ordeal for the young woman's family. I hope that a DNA test will provide a definitive answer, perhaps even prove his innocence; yes, I hope so, because if he was capable of murder, the void threatens once more, vast and gaping and ready to be flooded with innumerable new questions. Once again, it will be up to the law to decide. I am not fighting the truth, but the fall.

It's dizzying.

I'll have to go and see him in prison, even though so many people have warned me not to. I need to. I haven't been alone with him since we walked into the police station together five years ago.

When you looked at me in the morning, was there not a single moment when you felt pity for me?

Did you never think, 'I must stop'?

Did you abuse our daughter? Did you commit the most abject crime of all?

Do you have any idea of the hell we're living in? I will never forgive you for dragging our children and grandchildren into this suffering.

The night you came home crying, was that the night you tried to rape that young woman?

Why did you not talk about it?

Did you kill? Were you capable of killing?

I'll ask him all these questions. I need answers; he owes me that much. I will talk to the man I used to think I was married to. If he is still there, he will answer me. What does he have to lose, given that he is going to spend the rest of his life in prison? And if, in fact, that man vanished a long time ago, if all that remains of him is his pathological need for power and manipulation, I will sense that too. Either way, it will help me move on. This visit will not be an act of kindness nor a show of weakness, it will be a farewell and an essential stage in my recovery.

During a break in proceedings in the course of the Nîmes appeal, the Avignon police chief, Jérémie Bosse-Platière, who oversaw the investigation after Dominique's arrest, came to see me. 'I wanted to tell you how happy I am that you are doing okay.' He shook my hand for a long time; he didn't let go, as if my palm in his might finally cleanse his mind of my unconscious body, of the atrocities he had been forced to watch. I know this experience still haunts those who were tasked with gathering evidence for the investigation, and I owe them my life. And I know it still haunts the journalists who had the gruelling task of reporting on the lengthy trial. I owe it to them that I did not have to face my tormentors alone. When my lawyers announced my decision to hold the trial in public, journalists from all over the world turned up in huge numbers to report on what was unfolding. And it was so much more than a procession of monsters: it was a deep dive into all of us, ordinary men and women, into our bedrooms, our relationships, our families, our sewers. This story stirs up our violence, our barely concealed sordidness, our dormant traumas, our silences, our equivocations. It is the grubby reflection of the domination and predatory activity that still structure our world.

Now it's over. The case is closed. The rapists are all in prison. The man who appealed was sentenced to ten years instead of the original nine. The legal process is complete. It helped me and it tested me. It dissected fifty years of my life – half a century taken apart, undermined, and now receding into the past. It gave me allies for life, my lawyers Stéphane and Antoine. The daily phone calls over the last few years, all our questions, all their advice and encouragement – I cannot imagine our conversation ending with the closure of the case. All these aspects of the trial helped create an extended family around me, and I feel deeply connected to those who supported me when I had nothing left.

I love that word, family. It is the realm of my suffering and my healing. And at its heart, at the very heart of what I expected from life when I was young, there will always be my children and grandchildren, whom I love and miss so much. This story is theirs too. One day they will realise that our lives begin long before we do. I hope I'll be there to answer their questions in person. I will tell them that I kept the name Pelicot so that they need not be ashamed of it. I will tell them how much I loved taking the train to go and stay with them during the school holidays. I even believe that they saved me. Whenever I boarded the high-speed train to Paris, I was not the person who, only a few years earlier, had gone to work every weekday morning in EDF's nuclear department. I felt as if I was declining, at constant risk of a relapse. I was afraid of the blackouts I kept having, afraid that I had a brain tumour and was going to die. The truth is, the chemical submission didn't last ten or twelve hours: it affected every minute of my life.

I had no idea then, but I was only safe when I went away to take care of them. I was leaving the house of horrors. I embraced their lightness and also their concerns – tiny for us adults but so important to them. I gave my grandchildren the time and patience that we had not always had for our own children, and through them I savoured the delight of being six, seven, eight years old, the ages at which all I had done was wait for my mother to die. I thought I was watching over them. I realise now that it was they, albeit unawares, who were watching over me. Childhood, their childhood, became my refuge. My own, I realise, as I write these pages, is a strange little sanctuary I carry within me – holding both my solace and my sorrow. That is why my tears fall inward. With this book, I want to etch into that hidden place what happened to me afterwards. And to say that I am no longer afraid of being alone, that now I am able to fall asleep in the dark, a great victory. To say that we are reborn from our ashes, that I am alive, that I have rediscovered my *joie de vivre*, that I love Jean-Loup and that I regularly go to place flowers on his wife's grave, for the present does not erase the past.

I still need to believe in love. I received it intensely and too briefly from my parents, and for a long time I believed that it protected me from everything. I even believed that I knew how to give it.

I now know that it comes from a deep wound within me that makes me vulnerable. But I accept that fragility, that risk, still. To fight the emptiness, I need to love.

Gisèle Pelicot was named as the most noteworthy person of 2024 in an opinion poll in France, eclipsing world leaders, and was honoured by *Time*. To mark International Women's Day, the *Independent* named her the most influential woman of 2025.

Her case contributed to the national debate on sexual violence in France, which led to a change in the legal definition of rape.

She has been awarded the Légion d'honneur, France's highest civic honour.

Judith Perrignon is an award-winning novelist, journalist and essayist. She has helped several prominent French figures tell their stories, including Holocaust survivor Marceline Loridan-Ivens.

Natasha Lehrer is a prize-winning writer, translator and editor. Her journalism and book reviews have appeared in the *Guardian*, *Observer*, *Times Literary Supplement*, *Nation* and *Fantastic Man*, among others. She has contributed to several books, including a chapter on France in *Looking for an Enemy: 8 Essays on Antisemitism*, edited by Jo Glanville.

The writers she has translated include Neige Sinno, Nathalie Léger, Chantal Thomas, Vanessa Springora, Amin Maalouf, Victor Segalen, Robert Desnos and Georges Bataille. Her translations have been shortlisted and longlisted for several translation prizes, and she won the 2016 Scott Moncrieff Prize for *Suite for Barbara Loden*.

Ruth Diver is an award-winning literary translator and the former head of comparative literature at the University of Auckland, where she also taught French and Russian. She holds a PhD in French language and literature from the University of Paris 8, is the author of *Enfants russes, écrivains français: Nathalie Sarraute, Romain Gary*, and has published research on translingual authors in *Roman 20-50*,

Europe: Revue littéraire mensuelle and *Revue des lettres modernes*.

She won the Asymptote Close Approximations Fiction Prize in 2016 for her translation of *Maraudes* by Sophie Pujas and has since published over a dozen full-length translations, including *The Little Girl on the Ice Floe* by Adélaïde Bon and *A History of the Big House* by Charif Majdalani. Extracts from her translations have appeared in *Granta*, *Tripwire* and *Guernica*. She lives in Aotearoa, New Zealand.